HOME CHILDCARE
—— *vs* ——
CHILDCARE CENTERS

ALICE O. CARRILLO

Copyright © 2023 Alice O. Carrillo.

All rights reserved. No part of this book may be reproduced, stored, or transmitted by any means—whether auditory, graphic, mechanical, or electronic—without written permission of both publisher and author, except in the case of brief excerpts used in critical articles and reviews. Unauthorized reproduction of any part of this work is illegal and is punishable by law.

ISBN: 979-8-88640-755-6 (sc)
ISBN: 979-8-88640-756-3 (hc)
ISBN: 979-8-88640-757-0 (e)

Because of the dynamic nature of the Internet, any web addresses or links contained in this book may have changed since publication and may no longer be valid. The views expressed in this work are solely those of the author and do not necessarily reflect the views of the publisher, and the publisher hereby disclaims any responsibility for them.

One Galleria Blvd., Suite 1900, Metairie, LA 70001
1-888-421-2397

CONTENTS

Chapter 1	Home Childcare vs Childcare Centers	1
Chapter 2	A Home Provider: What She Offers a Child	5
Chapter 3	Owner of a Day Care	10
Chapter 4	My Own Opinion: Home Childcare VS Childcare Centers	15
Chapter 5	Why it is Important to be Trained and Experienced in Child Care	19
Chapter 6	Ideas on How to Ease Your Child's Anxiety About Childcare	25
Chapter 7	Injury Prevention	29
Chapter 8	Parent Handbook	34
Chapter 9	Parent/Child Care Contract	38
Chapter 10	Need Assessment Forms	40
Chapter 11	Every Day Outdoor/Indoor Activities	48
Chapter 12	Simple Science Activities You Can Do At Home	52
Chapter 13	Simple Curriculum Themes For Each Month For You And Your Child	55
Chapter 14	My Favorite Children Books	79
Chapter 15	Activities For Your Infant	82
Chapter 16	Child Care Home Programs Observations	85
Chapter 17	Child Development Centers Observations	93

Chapter 18 Observation Results 100
Chapter 19 The Importance of Childcare in a
            Home Environment Setting 104
Chapter 20 Health & Safety Issues 106
Chapter 21 Safety At Home 112
Chapter 22 Conclusion 114

CHAPTER 1

HOME CHILDCARE VS CHILDCARE CENTERS

The experiences with children has been truly rewarding throughout the years. It has brought many challenging moments that I wouldn't trade for anything. I decided to write this book because I feel that parents are not being informed on how to select the best childcare for their children. As many years of experience that I have had with children, I believe that childcare in a home environment, which provides a preschool program, is the best care your child can have. In the past years, I have had the opportunity of being a preschool teacher, a director of a childcare center, a home provider, owner of a Child Development Center and went on to earn a Masters in Early Childhood Development. Out of all my experiences, being a home provider has been the most challenging and rewarding. Throughout the book I will be explaining why I feel that home childcare with a preschool is the best for your child. I hope that by the time you finish reading this book you will agree. Home childcare provides a child with a family orientate environment. The child receives the motherly love, family values and safe pre-school experiences.

ALICE O. CARRILLO

Director of a Child Development Center

I became a director of a center in Salinas, California. Being a director not only is to keep the center under compliance with the state rules and regulations, but it also meant to keep up with the enrollment, accounts, program development, parent education workshops, monthly parent meetings, staff development, staff meetings, food programs, problems that incur throughout the day and interaction with children. It was a big responsibility!

Being under compliance with the state was very important. I had to check if the teacher/child ratio was not over what the state required. I also checked to see if there were any torn carpets where people could trip and get injured, holes where children played, broken toys or equipment. To our program, safety was our number one concern with the children, staff and parents.

Enrollment had to stay pretty consistent. If one child terminated we had to pick another quickly, in order to continue receiving funds. More children meant more funding.

My accounts were simple. Some parents paid a minimum fee, which was based according to their earnings plus any additional family members. They had to show proof, that during the weekend they paid day care because of their jobs. Most of out parents worked in the fields, so they also worked some weekends all year around. I never dealt with monies, only with receipts. Parents would drop the receipts off at the office and I would record them. The main office did the majority of the accounts. They received the funds and they also distributed them.

Program development was fun. I had to develop different programs for the center that were of interest to the children. One program that stands out in my mind is the "Tooth Program". Local dentists were invited to do presentations for the children. They would present a puppet show emphasizing the importance of mouth hygiene. They also distributed tooth brushes, and small toys to each child plus a free examination. The children enjoyed it a lot!

The Parent Education Program was also fun and challenging. I had to contact local agencies for help. For example: The Health Department would send professionals to talk about communicable and childhood diseases, nutrition and hygiene, this was a big plus with the parents.

Parent meetings were held once a month. This was a time to discuss concerns that the parents had about the program, which included the staff and children.

Staff Development was an area of importance to me. I felt that if the staff was not trained properly in early child development, the children would suffer. I brought excellent professionals to train my staff. When I had a properly trained staff, my children seemed to thrive in learning and positive attitudes.

Staff meetings were held once a week. This was a time to discuss any concerns that the staff had. Once a week meetings were a must. I felt that by having these meetings, it kept all my staff on top of things. By this, they were informed about all the new policies that were being implemented into the program. This was a good time to remind them that children are fragile and must be held and touched gently, as well as being treated with love and dignity. This insured a positive environment.

I had to keep a daily attendance for the Food Program. This meant I had to visit each classroom and see if the children were recorded on the daily attendance. This procedure was very important because the program received monies from the government to feed the children. If a child was not recorded, the program would not get paid.

Throughout the day, I would find time to talk with the children and ask questions about their day. My responsibility was to see that the children were in a safe learning environment.

A director is paid a monthly salary, which means if you worked over-time there is no compensation. I usually worked from 10 to 12 hours a day, in order for my program to operate smoothly. Even though directors do not get paid what they are worth, it is still quite a challenging profession!

I would arrive at work at approximately 6:30a.m. Continued working until 6:30-7:00p.m. On the following page I have included one of my regular scheduled days at a center that had from approximately 125 children.

Director's Schedule

6:30 A.M.	Open Center
6:30-8:00 A.M.	Greeting the parents and children
8:00-9:00 A.M.	Breakfast (supervise)
9:30-11:00 A.M.	Visit classrooms
11:00-12:00 noon	Lunch (supervise)
12:00 noon- 2:00 P.M.	Office: telephone calls, accounts, Monthly reports, and food program.
2:00-2:45 P.M.	Lunch
2:45-5:30 P.M.	Greeting parents
5:30-7:00 P.M.	Late pick ups

As you can see, my day was full and not a minute wasted. Even though some days were tiresome, I enjoyed my work. Being a director of a childcare center gave me the opportunity to learn the business, and was able to implement it into my own successful childcare business.

CHAPTER II

A HOME PROVIDER: WHAT SHE OFFERS A CHILD

A home provider offers services such as a substitute mother and a teacher to children that do not have any choice but to be in childcare. Today's economy has forced a high percentage of mothers to return to work. One of the biggest problems this nation faces today is "childcare". So it is up to the home provider to offer an excellent family orientated child care program, plus a safe learning environment for children.

A home provider must be trained and experienced in Early Child Education (ECE) or they cannot offer high quality child care. There is no way a person can develop a high quality program if they do not know anything about it! It is just like a person trying to build a house with no knowledge of how to build it!

Never enroll your child with a person that is not trained and experienced in Early Childhood Education and not licensed, or you will be facing big problems later. As days pass you will find many problems occurring, that usually do not occur with a home provider that is licensed and trained in Early Childhood Education. Problems that you will be confronting will be overcrowding, yelling, children that are ignored throughout the day and not being fed properly.

There are many home providers that are licensed, but not trained and experienced in Early Childhood Education; remember that! When you interview a home provider, ask if she has any training and experience, visit the program and observe her in action. If the home provider shows a lot of attention to the children and has an organized preschool program then 9 out of 10 she is an excellent provider.

A home provider provides "motherly love" to your child while you are at work. That is what I like about being a home provider; you treat the children like your own. If the child does not feel good, the provider is there to comfort him/her or if the child feels frustrated because "mommy" had to leave to work, the provider is there to comfort the child. Remember your home provider spends more time with your child then you do!

The teacher/child ratio is low compared to a center. If the home provider has 12 children enrolled in her program, the ration would be 6 to 1 because the requirement is that she has to have an assistant, whereas in a center it is 12 to 1 if a teacher has credentials. A home provider is able to give one on one attention, more than a teacher in a center.

Being a home provider is quite a rewarding profession. We are able to be mothers to precious children, plus teach because of all the training we earned in school. A home provider offers a tremendous support to a child that is having a problem at home. For example: a child that has parents that are going through a divorce, a home provider is there to comfort that child by hugging and holding the child, treating the child like one of her own. A provider can also explain to the child that mommy and daddy still love him/her and that it is not his/her fault the parents are separating. Maybe the provider will take the child for a walk and have a one-on-one discussion about how they are feeling and what is happening at home. The home provider insures the child that everything is going to be fine and that mommy and daddy still love him/her no matter what happens. The home provider also insures the child that they are there should the child need her.

Being a home provider is a challenging job. There is never a boring moment. You are always busy; cooking for the children or doing preschool, or maybe just sitting around talking and laughing with the children.

Home childcare offers a child a place where he/she can also call home. Another place he/she can go and feel comfortable, relaxed and free to play and explore in a safe learning environment.

A center is a structured place where there is certain criterion that must be met each day. They have a schedule that must be followed each day or else everything falls behind and becomes chaos.

At a home childcare the program runs smooth because we are not under pressure to finish a certain project that day. We can continue throughout the week and send it home on Friday.

Home childcare programs are not required to write up lesson plans like centers. Home providers use monthly curriculums which are not specific as lesson plans. The monthly curriculum is very general but gives enough information to a provider to follow for their preschool program. Plus she can add her own ideas.

Home providers do not dress business-like as a teacher would at a center. A provider can wear tennis shoes, pants and blouse or a jogging outfit. They dress comfortably and do not have to worry about a "dress code". This makes a child feel more comfortable because when mommy gets home from work, she changes into comfortable clothes. The child relates to this and accepts the environment which he is placed in much easier.

In home childcare, a child can bring their favorite blanket, toy, pillow or their favorite book. They can come in their pajamas and dress later if he/she does not feel well. Children can lay around all day if they prefer, especially when they feel ill. The provider is there to comfort and help the child to relax.

In home childcare the child has a choice of what he/she wants to do. The provider offers activities to the child. She sets them up and gives the opportunity for the child to choose what they want to do first. If the child does not feel like doing anything, it is all right with the provider. The child is not forced to participate, but is encouraged to try.

Overall, a home provider is a person that is sensitive toward the child's needs. She offers high quality childcare with a preschool program, plus well balanced meals. A home provider is a jack-of-all-trades: she is a mother, teacher, nurse, grandmother or just a friend. But most of all, she is there to offer family values.

Family values are fading away within family units because of the fact more mothers have to work long hours. The economy has forced mothers to leave their homes and place their children in day care from 12 to 15 hours a day. The home provider is there to provide family values through interaction with the children, making them feel like they are part of her family. How does a home provider do this? She gets the children involved in family activities. For example: serving a family style lunch, letting the children sit all together and having the children pass the serving bowls and serve themselves. A home provider discusses how important it is to sit together and eat. Another example is a cooking experience; having the children mix ingredients and talk with their friends, washing their utensils and bowls and straightening their area. Their activities help develop self-esteem, responsibilities, respect, caring, sharing, direction and sense of belonging.

Other examples are: watching a video together and discussing it, going for a walk or talking about his family and comparing to the family at childcare. Having a special name for the home provider – all my children called me "mama" instead of Teacher Alice. They relate me with their own mother at home. I think it is great! It is the warm approach by the children that makes me feel the love we share among ourselves.

Family values are so important, considering how the world is today. There is so much violence everywhere and it all falls on the lack of family values. Somewhere along the way, family values diminished. I feel that maybe it is because so many mothers are forced to work long hours, leaving their children alone or with babysitters that are not licensed and do not care about the well-being of the children.

The economy has taken mothers that prefer to be home with their little ones, go out and work in order to survive. A home childcare that is licensed and trained in Early Childhood Education knows that family values are important. They implement their own family values into their program. They feel that children need to be guided and explained why or why not this is not done or said around childcare. The provider feels that maybe when the children leaves to go home that he/she will take what he learned and continue to use it in their own home environment.

Family values are retained in childcare because of the fact that business is held in the provider home. To the provider, her home and family are the most important aspect in her life. She implements her own family values into her childcare because she cares and wants the children to practice good family values that are taught in her program.

Remember children stay with the provider longer hours then in their own proper home, which is why it is important to search for references when deciding what is best for your child. You must decide if the home provider is considerate toward your child and if her family is important to her. How do you find this out? By asking questions. You need to ask who lives there and if they have had a life scan done. What is their family like? Example: do they like family gathering, barbecue, picnics, etc.? Do any of them smoke or drink?

Do they like dancing or going out on Saturdays? Who else visits the home during the day? If you ask questions you will find out if that is the place you want your child to be ten or fifteen hours a day. By asking questions you will get an over all feeling whether it's negative or positive.

The provider that is trained in ECE and takes pride in her business, nine out of ten times, has excellent references from former clients. They do not hesitate to give you names of parents that have been in their program. An excellent provider loves it when you are concerned about your child. As a parent, you must not feel like you are being strict when asking questions. As a parent, you have the right to ask!

CHAPTER III

OWNER OF A DAY CARE

Prior to owning my own child development center, I was a home provider for ten years. There is a difference between the two. A home provider offers childcare in their home; and childcare center offers a childcare in a public building. The owner does not live on the premises.

My center was operated more like my childcare program. Although the rule and regulations were different, my learning environment was the same.

I had a house in a residential area in which I converted into a center. It had three bedrooms, two baths, a family room, and a living room. The bedrooms were quit large. The backyard was also large, which was an advantage. I had equipment inside and outside appropriate to age groups.

Having a big brother or sister in the same program helps the child to accept, becoming easier for them and for us to work with. Especially with children that have never had the experience of child care. Just seeing their sister or brother makes them feel good and lowers their anxiety.

My center was not structured like a center that is operated out of a building or a large meeting hall. My center was structured more like a house where children could come and feel free to explore and play. My children never felt they were going to a school to learn, they felt they were coming to my house to play and have fun. One thing that I emphasize with my parents was that they were not to call my place a "school" because I felt that children did not need to feel that they were attending school, especially being so young.

One thing that I will never approve of is chilcare care on school grounds for school age children. I feel that children do not need to be in school fifteen hours a day. Children need to have a different atmosphere after school is over. I feel that children that attend "center" in schools, churches, and public buildings all go through a burn out period sooner or later. School age children need a place where they can go after school, a home, and be free to take off their shoes, have snacks, play or do activities if they feel like it. Children do not need a structured place fifteen hours a day and then to be around a school setting after school hours.

The Food Program is provided so that the children can have nutritional meals and snacks each day. Every home provider qualified is able to receive monies every month to buy food for their program. There is no reason your child should not receive nutritional meals everyday. Ask your home provider about the food program. Ask to see her menus and maybe drop by during lunch time and see what she is serving that day. It is very important that your child is fed properly because, after all, your child is spending most of the day in the care of others. Remember that without nutrition your child will not grow physically and mentally. So it is very important for you to know what he eats daily!

Menu:

Breakfast:
Monday: Milk, peaches, corn flakes
Tuesday: Muffin, apple sauces, milk
Wednesday: Toast bread, scrambled eggs, pears, milk
Thursday: Watermelon, cherrios, milk
Friday: Oat meal, apples, milk

Lunch:
Monday: Cheese pizza, orange slices, peas, milk
Tuesday: Chicken soup, apple slices, crackers, milk
Wednesday: Bean burritos, green salad, watermelon slices, milk
Thursday: Beef Tacos, pears, Spanish rice, milk
Friday: Tuna Sandwich, kiwi, green salad, milk

Snack:
Monday: Yogurt, strawberries, water
Tuesday: Cottage cheese, pineapple bits, apple juice
Wednesday: Cheese, crackers, orange juice
Thursday: Apple slices, toast bread, grape juice
Friday: 100% fruit bar, water

The daily menu – it shows that for breakfast your child should have at least one serving per each area of milk product, bread, cereal and fruit. For lunch and dinner, a child must have one serving of the five food groups: milk, meat, vegetables and fruit, bread and cereal.

For afternoon snacks, your child should have at least one serving of two food groups. Children must be served milk every day for breakfast, lunch and dinner, if you are serving dinner. At the end of the month, the provider sends all of the menus, daily attendance on a monthly report to the state. Then the state reimburses the provider with monies for all the meals she served the children n under her care.

Another area, as an owner of a center that I thought was ridiculous, was the children and staff insurance. I could never find one that was not highly priced. There is a variety of insurance but not one that covered all areas I was concerned about. As owner of a center you were required to have full coverage for children and staff, and that was expensive. As a home provider you are not required to have insurance, as long as your parents sign the affidavits form. The form must be in the children's files at all times, signed and dated. As an owner of a center all of the responsibility fell on me. I was the owner and director of my program. I had to hire people that were qualified to teach children, meaning they had to have units in Early Childhood Education. It was difficult to find qualified people. As a home provider you are not required to have Early Childhood Education units, but I have always enforced it in my program because of the fact that parents prefer to send their children to a program that is well trained, experienced and organized in Early Childhood Education.

Another area that was different between centers and home childcare care is that private centers do not qualify for the food program put out by the state and federal government. So eventually it became expensive for me to continue to feed the children nutritional meals. As a home provider you qualify for the Food Program plus Children Food Network.

Children's Food Network, which are connected to the Food Bank, is an extra program that helps you with nutritional foods, enabling you to feed the children well balanced meals at low cost to you.

Equipment at a center was another area that had to be in excellent condition at all times, to where in home childcare they will let you slide by if your equipment was a little worn out. As a home provider we were given a notice to get a certain toy or equipment fixed by a certain date – if not done, licensing would force you to get rid of the object. We were not told to get rid of it right there and then and replace it with a new piece as they do at centers. Maybe because most centers are funded through the state and licensing knows they have funding for replacing worn out equipment, and home childcare does not have funding for replacing equipment.

Day Care Referral Agencies

Every county has a day care referral agency. These agencies offer free services to you. They receive all license child care providers' names and addresses from the Social Services Department of Licensing. The referral agencies categorize them by area and services they offer.

When you call, say exactly what your needs are, so that they can refer you to the best home provider in your area. The referral program not only offers day care referrals but also many other services. They can refer you to counseling, health centers, social services, education, community agencies, etc.

Some referral programs have a toy lending library where you can become a member and be eligible to check out toys for your child. I think this is a great idea to be able to check out toys, it beats buying them. Every time you take your children with you to check out toys it makes them feel like its Christmas.

Getting new toys every two weeks, but yet not costing you a penny, is great! As a home provider I love utilizing the toy lending library. My children feel like it is Christmas twice a month. The children do not become bored of the toys because I rotate them pretty often.

CHAPTER IV

MY OWN OPINION: HOME CHILDCARE VS CHILDCARE CENTERS

As I explained in my last chapter, the responsibilities of being the owner and director of a center was tremendous compared to being a home provider. Also the over head expenses were over whelming. Paying the mortgage payment, utilities, food, staff, and materials for the program, left me with very little money at the end of the month.

As a home provider I didn't have the over head expenses because I lived in the house I was doing my child care business. If I cared for six children I didn't need an assistant.

I decided to return back as a child care provider, not because of all the responsibilities and over head expenses as the owner of a center, but because I enjoyed seeing the children interact with each other in small groups, plus siblings being able to play together regardless of their age. In a home program the ratio is very minimal compared to a center.

Please do not get me wrong about childcare care centers. They can be good as far as educating children and getting them ready for school, but home day care provides the children with education plus family values.

Home childcare provides a place where a child can call home, come from school and relax in a family environment setting. Remember that when I talk about home day care it is a day care that is licensed, demonstrates safety, a preschool program plus nutritional meals every day.

When I worked as a director of a child development center I found that the whole program for the children was to structured, every minute of the day was crucial, children and staff had a schedule to meet daily.

In the last chapter I explained the teacher/child ration, but I feel I need to go through it again with you so that if anything you will memorize it.

The teacher/child ratio in a center is different that home childcare. As a center the ratio is 1/12 if the teacher had a certificate. If the teacher had an assistant that had 6 units in each childhood education the ratio in the classroom went up to 2/24 but assistant could not be left alone with the children, but it happens more regularly than we think. So over-all a classroom could have 24 children per 2 adults.

In home childcare the ratio is 2/12-14 You must have 2 adults for 12-14 children. So as you can see, the ratio in home day care is quite small compared to the center.

I enjoy teaching children in small groups, you seem to keep their interest longer, and are easier to handle. You don't seem to get as frustrated as when you have a large group of preschoolers loosing interest because the teacher can't keep their attention due to that she has to many children in the group. A teacher cannot handle 12 children by herself, especially when they are busy doing an art project. The younger the child, the smaller the group, because the attention span is limited.

Home childcare has a smoother transition throughout the day compared to centers.

Children seem to except responsibilities much easier then a center, maybe because it's not emphasized as much. The children in a home day care know that they must do it automatically, because at home they help mommy get utensils or put them away when baking. Children also love to wash dishes. In childcare we give children the opportunity to wash dishes as long as they are well supervised. Centers tend to emphasize on rules they post in classroom, constantly. In home childcare we don't stress the rules as much, because it's a home environment setting. Family values are emphasize more often then rules.

Overall home childcare is much healthier for a child then a center. By healthier, I mean mentally and physically. A child accepts childcare much faster in home childcare than at a center. I believe the reason is because of the home environment setting that they are put in. They relate it to their own home life. At a center they feel they are at a school all day, so therefore, they become frustrated after being in the same structured setting for 6 months, and doing the same basic schedule day in and day out. Children start being hyperactive, they don't want o listen to their teacher, they start to feel unwanted by their families and they start to hit other children for no apparent reason.

All these problems start to sprout when a child becomes unhappy in a structured environment. A young child gets the burnout syndrome much faster than an older child. Remember that here I'm talking about children that are in a normal range. Children that all of a sudden act up and you don't understand why.

Young children love to be free to do as they please. They love to be free to explore and feel comfortable about it. They love being in an environment that they can relate to their own family life at home I believe children in home childcare can receive the motherly love they deserve and yearn for. Home childcare providers are like "mother figures", more than "teacher figures", even though we teach children.

In home childcare children learn in a fun way. We provide them with opportunities and give them the choice of what they feel like doing at that moment. We are not pressured for time when doing art activities. If a child doesn't feel like doing the art activities that moment, then maybe he feels like doing it later, or maybe the following day.

Remember that preschool is a time to develop large and small muscles. It is a time to learn through dancing, and singing—not constant drilling and writing ABC"S and numbers. Preschool is a time children learn about nature, family, and friends.

Home childcare offers a child the right to live rather then to exist. In a home setting environment, children seem to be happier, because of the surroundings. They easily relate it to their own family life. The home setting helps children to accept responsibilities because they also have responsibilities at home.

You, as a parent, need to observe home childcare programs that do straight day care, so that you can also get a feeling of a program that does not practice preschool. Remember that there is a very minimal childcare program with preschool program that are excellent.

If you're looking for a childcare with maybe 3 to 4 children and maybe looking for a grandmother type that gives a lot of love and attention to you baby, then maybe that's the programs for you. Remember that your child sooner or later needs a childcare program that offers preschool.

CHAPTER V

WHY IT IS IMPORTANT TO BE TRAINED AND EXPERIENCED IN CHILD CARE

The most important aspect of child care: Is the home provider trained and experienced in child care? A home provider can be licensed without being trained or experienced, in early childhood education, so it's up to you as a parent to ask and seek references. Placing your child in a day care where there is no interaction with the children is an injustice to your child. By interaction I mean is there a preschool program in action, is there a variety of toys for children to play with inside and outside? Is the home big enough for your child to feel comfortable in? Does the home provider use teacher language with the children? Does the home provider seem to interact with the children by talking with them and involving herself in role playing? Make a surprise visit. It's the only way you will find out.

An excellent child care program includes the following:

1. Safety: Are the children in a safe environment? Is there to many people going in an out all day long? Is the house packed with a

lot of things? Is the house dirty? Are things thrown around to where you child can get injured.

2. Nutrition: Is the child care program in the Food Program? Look at the menu, are
The meals balanced. Check and see what your child ate today (breakfast, lunch & snack)

3. Health & Hygiene: Are the children clean? Do the children have runny noses? Does the provider use a clean tissue when cleaning the child's nostrils every time?
Is the provider implementing health issues into her daily routine?

4. Respecting the child: Is there any put downs by the provider to the children?
Is she treating the children equal?

5. Pre-school: Is the program providing activities and toys to the children?
Are the toys and equipment age appropriate?

When a home provider says, "I am qualified to take care of your child because I raised five children of my own." You ask, "In what ways?" Do you have early childhood education training?" If she answers, "No", then you reply, "I guess you don't qualify."

As a parent, you will be taking a big risk in placing your child in a childcare that the home provider is not trained and experienced in early childhood education. I have seen so many programs out there that are not trained or experienced that give me the chills and as I leave I see children that are yearning for attention just by the way they look at me, and don't interact with the provider.

Children that are placed in day care like this do not grow mentally, and some don't grow physically, because of the lack of good nutritional meals and lack of exercise. Don't get me wrong, there are some programs that are strictly day care and give the attention and interaction that children need, but the lack of preschool is also important.

CPR is another area that you must find out if the provider has, by asking where is the certificate posted? You must check date and see if it's not expired. CPR stands for Cardio Pulmonary Recitation, which is training in breathing techniques for children and adults that experience choking, heart attacks, etc. The providers are certified for two years. After two years they have to retake the training in order to stay under compliance with the community care licensing department. It's very important for your caregiver to have this training, if she doesn't it is your right to call the department and report her.

Home providers can earn the CPR training through a local college, fire department, and hospitals. There is no excuse for a home provider not to have this training. I believe that all home providers must have this training because they are dealing with children that are not their own. I also believe that the worst experience a home provider can encounter is a child that is choking and not know what to do, causing the child to die. The training is simple, anyone can pass the training. They are offered in English and Spanish.

You as parent should take CPR Training also. It's the best gift you can give to your child. It should be a law that all new parents take the CPR Training. It saves lives!

Call your local Child Care Resource and Referral, Family Day Care Association or a support group in your area. These organizations have a list of child care providers that they can refer to you. These organizations break down what these child care providers offer. You might be looking for a provider that has license and a pre-school program. Maybe you want a small group setting or just a grandmother that can give a lot of attention to your baby. These organizations can give you the break downs of each childcare provider that suits your needs.

The following questions you must ask the child care provider you are interviewing. Remember these questions will help you select a high quality child care for your precious child.

1. Are you licensed through community care licensing?
2. Do you have references that I can call and ask them about your program?
3. Do you have any early childhood training?
4. Is your CPR current?
5. Do you belong to the state Food Program?
6. Do you post your menu where parents can see it?
7. Do you have any large animals in the back yard?
8. Do you smoke or drink liquor?
9. Do you have a pre-school program?
10. How many adults live in your home?
11. Have all the adults taken fingerprints?
12. Do you have an assistant?
13. Does your assistant know where the emergency numbers are posted and the children files are?
14. Does your assistant have the CPR training?
15. Does your assistant have training in early childhood education?
16. Do you have a car?
17. Does your assistant have a car?

Nutrition is another concern you should be aware of. Is the child care provider receiving funds from the Food Program? These funds enable the provider to offer nutritional meals and snacks to your child. Talk with her and ask her if she is a member of the Food Program. Also, ask her if you can see her menus, so that you can see what she serves throughout the week. A lot of providers do not post the menus but they have them in their files. Ask your child if they had candy that day, if the child is having candy every day, that tells you your child is not having nutritional meals. Be aware that there are providers that belong to the Food Program, but yet they do not serve nutritional meals. They like the money they are receiving, but they are not serving well balanced meals and snacks. As a parent, be very careful in finding a provider that does follow the rules in all areas.

Infant Care is also another big concern to me. The majority of providers today, do not have the Infant Care Training Program offered at your local college. Infant Care offers the provider training on how to take care of infants from CPR to handling an infant, feeding, diaper changing, and hygiene. The provider must be able to give a lot of tender love and care to the infant through nurturing.

If the provider is not able to give at least the tender loving care an infant needs then she is not worthy of taking care of you infant. If you cannot find a provider that is trained in Infant Care, then your next step is to hire a provider that is loving and shows concern toward your baby. As soon as your baby starts to walk terminate you child from the program and put him/her in another child care that offers a pre-school program. Remember that learning and growing is important for you child.

Always visit a child care program during the day when children are interacting with each other. The best time is between 9:00a.m.-12:00p.m. or 3:00p.m.-5:00p.m.

Visiting a program when children are asleep, is not very smart. Children will sleep 12:30p.m.- 3:00p.m. During nap time the children are asleep and you will miss the interacting your child was involved in. If you want to see your child active then you must visit the program during activity time.

The following is the "How to Discipline the Children:" If the provider does not have the discipline rules posted then you must share them with her. I like to see the Discipline Steps taken by Joanne Hendrick, the author of the Whole Child. Here they are:

1. Warning him/her
2. Removing him from the activity while keeping him with the teacher
3. Acknowledge feelings and stating rules
4. Waiting for him to make the decision to return to the activity.
5. Helping him return and be successful

Joanne believes children need to be taken through all five steps in order to develop self-esteem. If your provider does not have the discipline steps, please share them with her. Explain to the provider this is the professional way to discipline the children and that you would be more than happy to give her "How to Discipline the Children" by Joanne Henderick. Tell her she must post them on the wall where parents can see the procedures. Also tell her to write them on poster board using big letters so that parents and children can see them clear.

CHAPTER VI

IDEAS ON HOW TO EASE YOUR CHILD'S ANXIETY ABOUT CHILDCARE

The following are some ideas that you can do to help develop your child's growth and help you child function normal at child care. These pointers will help you easing the pressure of child care for you and your child.

1. Let your child know that you are going to work but that you will be back to pick him/her up. Reassuring your child is like telling him to relax and have fun.
2. Always hug and kiss your child before leaving every morning to work.
3. Let your child know that you are there for him. Tell him that the provider has your work number if he feels the need to call.
4. Encourage your child to seek reasonable ways on how to get adults to listen if he has something to say.
5. Help your child to become a leader not a follower by telling him that no one can make him do something he doesn't feel comfortable doing.
6. always encourage your child to try a new skill and praise the accomplishments.

7. Ask your child questions about his day. What they did, who visited, etc.
8. Spend quality time with your child on your days off.
9. Send a picture of the family in your child's backpack, so that your child can see it during the day.
10. Eat lunch with your child at child care or pick your child up and treat him to lunch. Go to the park and eat your lunch. Do this at least once a month.
11. Take your child to work and show your child where you work and what you do.
12. Praise you child's art work, place the work somewhere the child can see it.
13. Take pictures of your child's child care friends and make your child an album so that he can see them when he is home.
14. Take your child to grocery store. Buy fruit and have your child share with the child care children.
15. Take a day off from work and spend it at child care, helping at the child care, giving your child one to one attention.
16. Invite the child care family for a potluck or barbecue. This gives you the opportunity to meet your child's child care family.
17. Share telephone numbers with your child's child care families.
18. Invite your child's child care family for an outing and talk about the children discussing what the children do at child care.
19. On your child's birthday buy a cake or take cake mix and the children can have cooking experience and afterward sing the birthday song to your child.
20. Have an arts and crafts day at your home and invite the child care families.
21. Volunteer during a field trip. Gives you a chance to spend time with your child.
22. Buy pizza and take it to the child care and share it with the children.
23. Take family pictures to the childcare and share them with the other children.

24. Eat breakfast with your child at child care. Eat whatever they are serving
25. Read at night to your child. Substitute name of his child care friends into the stories you're reading.
26. Have your child sing a song he learned at child care.
27. Encourage the child to keep a journal about his day. You ask and write down his adventures at child care.
28. Donate your old toys to the child care.
29. Invite one or two child care friends to stay the night at your place.
30. Encourage the child care families to rotate babysitting on weekends giving the parents time away from the children.
31. Take a walk with your child and talk about the child care friends.
32. last but not least, encourage your child to share and be kind to others.

If you do what I mentioned above I truly believe you will have a successful child, and as a parent you will feel comfortable in leaving him at child care.

The percentage of parents feeling guilty about leaving their child at child care is very high. This guilt affects the performance of work you do at your job. If you are not happy with the care your child is getting, don't hesitate to remove your child and seek care elsewhere. If you are feeling guilty because you are leaving your child long hours then perhaps you need to look at your own schedule. Ask yourself: Can I change shifts? Can I cut down my working hours? Can my husband or I change our schedules to where one of us can be there for Johnny half of the .

Now-a-days employers are sensitive to parents needs. They are finding that if employees are helped with child care problems, the employees are more productive at their jobs. Don't hesitate to talk with your boss for advice. Nine out of ten times he will be very understanding and will offer a helping hand.

With all the observations I have made, comparing centers to home child care, I came to the conclusion that there is nothing like home child care for any child. Home child care offers a child tender loving care, low child ratio, a safe home learning environment, family values, and a place your child can call a second home.

I hope that you will agree with me and follow up to seek a home child care program that is appropriate for your child and fits your needs. Use the checklist that I mentioned in the book to help you find a home child care that will satisfy your needs. I hope this book will be the best investment you have ever made because when it comes to your child's needs it should be a priority.

CHAPTER VII

INJURY PREVENTION

The following simple rules must be followed in order to prevent injury to your child. Share these with you child care provider, after all it keeps your child safe and makes you feel that your child is in a safe environment. Share this with your provider.

1. Purchase a Choke Tester so that you can test small objects that children can put in their mouths. If the object fits than you must throw it away, before it causes an injury to your child. Remember young children put everything in their mouths.
2. Throw away broken toys and equipment
3. Keep pins and nails, toothpicks, paper clips, tacks, staples locked up.
4. Pick up hazardous objects, and cleaning detergents and place them in a locked container.
5. Keep medicine in a locked cabinet.
6. Don't give Styrofoam cups to babies.
7. Don't wear long dangly jewelry.
8. Don't ever prop an infant's bottle when feeding.
9. Never leave a child unattended
10. Always check pacifiers to see if they are loose.
11. Don't let children run with things in their mouths. Don't let children put pencils in their mouths.

12. Don't feed babies raw vegetables and hard candies.
13. Train children to walk with pointed side of scissors in the palm of the hand.
14. Never let children us a stapler without supervision.
15. Never put hard candies in a piñata.
16. Don't ever have plastic swimming pools full of water.
17. Don't ever let children play with plastic bags.
18. Always be aware of toys on stairways, and thrown on the floor. Pick them up Immediately!
19. Always clean the floor from any water spilled.
20. Always take enough adults when going on a field trip.
21. Keep all children properly seated in your car with appropriate seat belts and car seats.
22. Get rid of all your poisonous plants indoor and outdoors.
23. Never have a child next to the stove.
24. Never let toddlers and preschoolers play with ropes.
25. Teach your child the 911 number. Explain to your child that he or she can only use it during emergencies.
26. Post the poison center telephone number on wall near telephone.
27. Have the children name and parents name and telephone # by your telephone
28. Teach you child about signal lights. Take your child for a walk and teach traffic safety rules.
29. Teach your child about fire safety. Teach your child to drop and roll on the floor. In case your child is on a fire teach him to crawl low and explain why. Teach your child if door is hot, do not open.
30. Teach your child about earthquake safety. Teach your child to get under table or door way.
31. Teach your child variety of ways to get out of the house, in case of a fire.
32. Teach your child to climb up and down stairs the right way.
33. Keep all household items up in high places.
34. Set your water heater to 120 degrees or less. Cover all electrical oulets.

35. If you have a toddler put a protection gate at the beginning of the stairs.
36. Check bath water before putting your child in. Best way to check water is with your elbow. After bathing make sure you let water drain out and not left in tub.
37. Never answer the phone while bathing your child.
38. Never put infant in bathtub without a restrainer.
39. If you have an infant keep the crib clean. Never leave toys in crib or plastic bags or small objects.
40. When traveling your infant must be in car seat not in your arms. Infant car carrier must be on the back seat facing the rear.
41. Keep cigarettes lighters, matches, and candles away from your child.
42. Always have your swimming pool covered or install a fence around it and lick it.
43. Teach your child where you keep your flashlight for in case of emergency.
44. Use safety locks in all cabinets in bathrooms, and kitchen.
45. Teach your child to use plastic glass when drinking liquids.
46. Teach your child how to swim at an early age.
47. Teach your child camping rules.
48. Before going camping check all equipment to see if they work properly.
49. When traveling keep a First Aid Kit in the car and other helpful items. Example: Flash light, flares, extra tire, blankets, towels and water.
50. Make sure walls at home are painted and patched u correctly. The walls should not be chipped.
51. Keep paint, petroleum, paint thinner, and anything toxic in your tool shed and keep it locked.
52. Teach your child the right way to handle his or her pet. If possible take dog to training classes.
53. If child goes somewhere without you, give him at least 25 cents so that he can call 911 or call you if an emergency occurs.
54. Teach your child to use the public phone.

55. Buy your child flame resistant clothes.
56. Cover your fireplace.
57. Keep all plastic bags, trash bags, shopping bags out of reach.
58. Keep all poisonous plants away from children. Parents tend to buy indoor plants without knowing that they are poisonous.
59. Take CPR and First Aid Class.
60. Take parenting classes.
61. If at all possible enroll in a preschool where you and your child can attend together.
62. Check your grass for hidden objects.
63. Plant outdoor plants that are not poisonous
64. Swings are dangerous for children. Make sure you are there to push you child Never let another child push a swing.
65. Outdoor furniture should not have sharp edges.
66. Make sure sprinklers are installed correctly and are not sticking out to far.
67. Always supervise your child when doing water activities. Buy Little Tyke equipment for the outdoors. I have found they are safe and attractive for children.
68. Indoor furniture should not have sharp edges. Furniture must be attached to wall
69. If you have an empty refrigerator or freezer you need to lock it.

The following is a list of poisonous plants: Share with your provider. Keep your eyes open for plants in the homes when you visit. Many plants are poisonous that we are not aware.

Hyacinth	Azalea
Tobacco	Philodendron
Baneberry	Daffodils
Ivy	Lily of the Valley
Jasmine	Black Locust
Mistletoe	Holly

Elephant ear
Shamrock
Iris
Buttercups

Potato Leaves
Tomato Leaves
Poinsettia
Mushrooms

The following is a list of safe plants: Share with your provider

Pussy Willow
Moss
Rose
Lilac
Honeysuckle
Boston
Pine cone Seeds
Wandering Jew

Rubber Plant
Begonia
Jade Plant
Spider Plant
Swedish Ivy
Fern Artichoke
Rubber Plant
Yucca

FOODS THAT CAUSE CHILDREN TO CHOKE AND SUFFOCATE

Hard candy
Lollipops
Gum
Popcorn
Raw Carrots
Raw Celery
Raw Apples
Peanuts

Chips
Hot Dogs
Peanut Butter
Raisins
Grapes with skin
Nuts
Cherries
Yogurt with nuts

CHAPTER VIII

PARENT HANDBOOK

Your childcare provider will give you a **Parent's Handbook.** The Parent's Handbook is one of the required booklets that a trained license child care provider will offer you when you become one of her clients. The handbook is full of general information about the providers program. It should include the admission procedures, fees, hours of operation, rules and regulations, attendance, Illness, emergency, vacations and holidays, components of the program, termination of services, nondiscrimination, rights of the program, toys, birthdays, pets, fields trips, clothing, nutrition, qualified staff, discipline rules, and conferences.

The following are forms that you must fill out before entering a child care program that are included in the Parent's Handbook.

Identification and Emergency Form

The Identification and Emergency Form (F-700) must be completed accurately by the parents. This form indicates to us the people to depend on in case of and emergency, providing the parents cannot be contacted first. The form also indicates who the Doctor is, what hospital is preferred and if there are any allergic reactions to medication.

Parents' Right Form

The Parents' Right Form (F-995) informs parents that they have the right to enter and inspect the child care facility their child is attending. It also gives the parent's the right to enter your home if they feel their child is in some kind of danger. The form must be posted where parents can see it.

Personal Rights Form

The Personal Rights Form (F-613) informs parents that they have the right to contact the Licensing Agency on any complaints they might have against the program in which their child is enrolled. The telephone number of the agency is on the form.

Consent for Medical Treatment Form

Consent for Medical Treatment Form (F-629) gives the provider the right to provide emergency medical care in order to preserve the life of the child that is under your care. This copy must be signed by the parents.

Affidavit Regarding Liability Insurance

The Affidavit's Regarding Liability Insurance (F-282) explains to parent that the provider has no liability insurance. The provider can ask you to use your medical insurance if needed.

Food Program Enrollment Form

The Food Program Enrollment form indicates the child on the form is participating in the food program. This form must be signed by parents or reimbursement will not be issued for the provider.

Child's Pre-Admission Health Evaluation Physician Report

The child's Pre-Admission Health Evaluation Physician Report (F85-378) indicates the child is in good health and is able to attend child care. It is the parent's responsibility to take the child to their family doctor for a thorough examination. The doctor signs the form and it is returned to the provider.

Parent's Report Form

The Parents" Report Form (F90-55707) helps to let a child care provider know a little about the child's background: what is the child's favorite food, what time is his regular meal time, what time does he nap, play experiences, special problems, and fears. The importance of this form is to make it easier for the child to cope with the anxiety of breaking away from parents and be able to accept child care.

Immunization Records Required

Parents must present a record of their child's immunizations before he or she can attend a child care program. The record must include the date (at least the month and year) of each vaccine dose was received. The immunization of each child must then be copied onto the blue California School Immunization Record available from your county health department, This record must be kept in the child's file and must be reviewed each month by the provider. If your child needs immunizations the provider will let you know.

Recommended Childhood Immunization Schedules

Age
2-3 months
4-5 months
6-14 months
15-17 months

4-6 years (before school entry)

Vaccines
Polio, DTP/DT, & Hib
Polio, DTP/DT & Hib
DTP/DT & Hib
MMR, Polio, DTP/DT & Hib
(MMR at 12 months, in some areas)
Polio, DTP/DT & MMR

Hepatitis B is recommended if your child attends a child care program. There is three series of shots that must be taken. The first one must be taken one month before the next one is taken. The second one must be taken six months before the third one.

Varicella (chicken pox) also recommended if child is attending a child car program.

Definition of Vaccine Codes

DTP Diphtheria and Tetanus toxoides, Pertussis Vaccine Absorbed

TD Tetanus and Diptheria Toxoides Absorbed

Polio Trivalent Oral Polio Vaccine

MMR Measles, Mumps, Rubella

Hib Haemophilus Influenza Type B Vaccine

CHAPTER IX

PARENT/CHILD CARE CONTRACT

Every parent should complete a contract. The contract specifies parent's names, social security number, driver's license, employment address and phone number, contract hours and weekly fee, and that the Parent's Handbook has been received. The contract covers the home provider if the parents decide to quit and do not pay. With the contract signed by both parents, the provider can prove in court that the children were registered in her program. Also the parents can prove that they were registered in the program for in case you take the provider to court for one reason or another.

Here is a copy of the contract:

PARENTS/CHILD CARE CONTRACT
PARENT'S NAME (S)_____
FATHER'S HOME ADDRESS_____
FATHER'S TELEPHONE #_____
FATHER'S EMPLOYMENT ADDRESS_____
FATHER'S EMPLOYMENT TELEPHONE #_____
FATHER'S DRIVER'S LICENSE #_____
FATHER'S SOCIAL SECURITY #_____
MOTHER'S HOME ADDRESS_____

HOME CHILDCARE VS CHILDCARE CENTERS

MOTHER'S TELEPHONE #_____
MOTHER'S EMPLOYMENT ADDRESS_____
MOTHER'S EMPLOYMENT TELEPHONE #_____
MOTHER'S DRIVER'S LICENSE #_____
MOTHER'S SOCIAL SECURITY #_____
CHILD'S NAME_____
CHILD'S BIRTHDATE_____
INITIAL CONTRACT DATE_____

CHILD CARE SERVICES CONTRACT:
HOURS_____
DAYS_____

IF CHILD IS NOT PICKED UP ACCORDIING TO CONTRACT HOURS, YOU WILL BE CHARGED_____ AN HOUR UNTIL PARENT ARRIVES FOR CHILD.

I_____HAVE RECEIVED THE PARENTS' HANDBOOK AND AGREE TO COMPLY WITH ITS REGULATIONS.
PARENT (S) SIGNATURE_____

CHILD CARE PROVIDER'S SIGNATURE_____
DATE_____

Remember it's important for you to answer every question. Also remember to read every question before answering it. These forms are used for in case of an emergency that might incur during child care hours. If your provider does not have these forms, recommend that she gets them from Social Services Community Care Licensing, by writing or calling them. .If she cannot provide you with these forms, more probable she is not license.

CHAPTER X

NEED ASSESSMENT FORMS

The following forms are for you, so that you can assess your child and see the development he is going through. I believe a child needs to be assessed up to four years old. After four years of age, the child is pretty well developed and you are aware of the child's needs. Remember this is not a standardized test—this is more of an observation technique. Some children will achieve earlier or later than others. Every child is unique in their development. These forms are just to give you some lead way of how your child is developing. You will know how he is developing in the areas of language, emotional, physical, social and cognitive skills, which will alert you if your child is slow in any area. This procedure will help you practice with your child in certain area so he will be able to master it on time.

NEED ASSESSMENT FORMS:
Share these forms with your daycare provider.
INFANT: LLEVEL 0-2 YEARS

Lift chin

Generally mastered at one month　　　　Age_____Date_____

Holds head up

Generally mastered at two months　　　　Age_____Date_____

Rolls from side to back
Generally mastered at three months   Age_____Date_____

Lifts head and chest up
Generally mastered at four months   Age_____Date_____

Rolls from stomach to stomach
Generally mastered at six months   Age_____Date_____

Plays with toes
Generally mastered at six months   Age_____Date_____

Sits up
Generally mastered at seven months   Age_____Date_____

Crawls forward and backward
Generally mastered at nine months   Age_____Date_____

Stands up alone
Generally mastered at twelve months   Age_____Date_____

Walks

Generally mastered at twelve months   Age_____Date_____

Two-three word sentences
Generally mastered at twenty months   Age_____Date_____

Identified pictures by pointing and naming them
Generally mastered at twenty months   Age_____Date_____

Matches identical objects
Generally mastered at twenty-four months   Age_____Date_____

PHYSICAL DEVELOPMENT: LEVEL 24-36 MONTHS

Walk on line
Generally mastered at twenty-four months Age_____Date_____

Can kick a ball
Generally mastered at twenty-four months Age_____Date_____

Jumps up with both feet
Generally mastered at thirty months Age_____Date_____

Climbs on equipment
Generally mastered at thirty-six months Age_____Date_____

Learn to ride a tricycle
Generally mastered at thirty-six months Age_____Date_____

Completes puzzles (3-4 pieces)
Generally mastered at thirty-six months Age_____Date_____

Enjoy finger painting
Generally mastered at thirty-six months Age_____Date_____

LANGUAGE ASSESSMENT: LEVEL 24-36 MONTHS

Speaking two-and three-word sentences
Generally mastered at twenty-to twenty-four months Age_____Date_____

Uses preposition
Generally mastered at thirty months Age_____Date_____

Memorizes at least one nursery rhyme
Generally mastered at thirty-six months Age_____Date_____

Starts to ask questions
Generally mastered at thirty-six months Age_____Date_____

COGNITIVE DEVELOPMENT: LEVEL 24-36 MONTHS

Answers by pointing or naming
Generally mastered at thirty months   Age_____Date_____
Matches colors
Generally mastered at thirty months   Age_____Date_____
Matches shapes
Generally mastered at thirty months   Age_____Date_____
Begins to group objects
Generally mastered at thirty-six months   Age_____Date_____
Able to identify objects in pictures
Generally mastered at thirty months   Age_____Date_____

SOCIAL/EMOTIONAL ASSESSMENT: LEVEL 24-36 MONTHS

Calls women and men "mommy and daddy" and children "babies"
Generally mastered at twenty-four   Age_____Date_____
months
Possessive with toys
Generally mastered at thirty months   Age_____Date_____
Interacts with others
Rarely_____Usually_____Always_____
Smiles and shows positive emotional responses
Rarely_____Usually_____Always_____
Explores with things
Rarely_____Usually_____Always_____
Is creative
Rarely_____Usually_____Always_____
Rating of self-esteem
Low_____Adequate_____High_____

PHYSICAL DEVELOPMENT ASSESSMENT: LEVEL 36-48 MONTHS

Hops on one foot

Generally mastered at forty-three months   Age_____Date_____

Stands on one foot

Generally mastered at forty-eight months   Age_____Date_____

Catches a ball

Generally mastered at forty-eight month   Age_____Date_____

Jumps with both feet together

Generally mastered by forty-eight months   Age_____Date_____

Responses positively to physical contact

Rarely_____Usually_____Always_____

Separates easily from parents

Rarely_____Usually_____Always_____

Positive feelings about himself

Rarely_____Usually_____Always_____

Explores new things

Rarely_____Usually_____Always_____

LANGUAGE ASSESSMENT: LEVEL 36-48 MONTHS

Tells what is happening on a picture

Generally mastered at thirty to forty months   Age_____Date_____

Knows basic colors

Generally mastered at thirty-six to forty months   Age_____Date_____

Tells stories

Generally mastered at thirty-six to forty-eight months   Age_____Date_____

Cuts paper with scissors

Generally mastered at forty-eight months   Age_____Date_____

Draws circles

Generally mastered at forty-eight months   Age_____Date_____

COGNITIVE DEVELOPMENT: LEVEL 36-48 MONTHS

Describes objects

Generally mastered at thirty-six to forty-eight months   Age_____Date_____

Is able to tell the difference between two objects

Generally mastered at thirty-six to fort-eight months   Age_____Date_____

Is able to put three objects in order by size

Generally mastered at thirty-six to forty-eight months   Age_____Date_____

Is able to put three objects in order by color

Generally mastered at thirty-six to forty-eight months   Age_____Date_____

Relates meaning to scribbles or drawings when asked

Generally mastered at thirty-six to forty-eight months   Age_____Date_____

SOCIAL/EMOTIONAL ASSESSMENT: LEVEL 36-48 MONTHS

Shares toys, takes turns
Generally mastered at thirty-six to forty-two months   Age_____Date_____

Begins to use words to express feelings
Generally mastered at thirty-six to forty-two months   Age_____Date_____

Has imaginary playmates
Generally mastered at forty-two to forty-eight months   Age_____Date_____

Explores new things
Rarely____Usually_____Always_____

Responds positively to physical contact
Rarely____Usually_____Always_____

Positive feelings about himself
Rarely____Usually_____Always_____

The following is some examples of what your child should know before he is accepted in kindergarten. Maybe share with your childcare provider. Ask her if she can teacher your child the following concepts.

Colors

Recite alphabets through music

Parts of the body

Parts of the face

Shapes

Concepts: Right and left, big and little

Numbers: 1-20

Full name: First & last

Home address

Telephone

Emergency number: 911

If you have time teach your child the recognition of upper and lower case ABC's

This however is not required.

CHAPTER XI

EVERY DAY OUTDOOR/ INDOOR ACTIVITIES

Here's some activities for you and your child to do. This will help you get involved with your child plus forcing your child to be active. Share these activities with your childcare provider.

Baseball

Kick ball

Get wet using the sprinklers

Washing dolls

Bubbles

Washing toys

Bike ride

Go to the park

Treasure hunting

Swimming

Plant a garden together

Building something together

Unscrew an appliance and put it back together. Makes sure the cords are cut off.

Bake cookies

Cook lunch together

Sing-a-long

Go for a walk

Four square (ball game)

Watch a video together

Make home made play dough together and play with it together

Plant flowers in your yard

Exercise with music

Dance with music and scarves

Invite your child's friends and play musical chairs

Invite your child's friends and have an outdoor picnic

Invite your child's friends and camp outdoors

ACTIVITIES FOR RAINY DAYS

Block Building

Paper tearing

Paper squeezing

Paper cutting

Walking on masking tape

Play dough

Cooking experience

Bean bags

Legos

Scavenger Hunt

Musical Chairs, Duck-Duck Goose, Simon Says, Seven Up Heads up

Dancing (Using scarves and yarn)

Exercise

Place butcher paper on table and let children be creative.

Sing-a-long—invite his friends to sing songs that are familiar to them.

Storytelling: Show picture and let children tell a story to the others.

Dressing the bears: Collect bears and baby clothes, let children dress the bears.

Make circles, triangle, squares, and rectangle using masking tape on the floor. Have the children walk to shapes and say them.

Jumping rope

Have your child tell you a story that he likes and knows

Put a family album together and have him carry it to day care and share.

Have your child cut out a clipping from newspaper, and tell you about it.

Discuss with your child what happened during the week—let him talk the most.

Involve your child in your daily planning. Have him give ideas as to what he wants to do during the day.

Games—play games with your child. Some games to play are Duck, Duck Goose, Hot

Potatoes, or Heads up 7-up.

Put objects in a bag-have your child feel the objects and guess what they are.

Rhythmic Body Movement—use an album that encourages body movement.

Teach your child how to read a calendar—teach him about days, weeks, months and years.

CHAPTER XII

SIMPLE SCIENCE ACTIVITIES YOU CAN DO AT HOME

Share with your childcare provider the following science activities. They are simple

And fun to do.

Make you own science kits: Rocks, pine cones, magnets, screws & bolts.

Old appliances with cords cut off: A couple of screwdrivers. Let children unscrew

the appliances

Large magnets and sand: Let children pick up pieces of medal in the sand

Water or pitcher plus glasses: Children can learn how to pour and measure

Ice cubes in bowl: Children experience and see how they melt.

Wash toys outside: Children love to do this on a warm day. Let them get wet.

Make bubbles: Use bubble bath and water. Let children blow bubbles.

Collect rocks: Different shapes and colors.

Pour salt in a box: Let children feel texture and draw with fingers.

Put water in a bucket: Have objects that float and objects that don't float

Put water in a bucket and give painting brushes: Children can paint the fence and see the change of the wood when using water.

Have a box with all sizes of screws and bolts: Children can screw the bolts together and unscrew the bolts. Remember no small screws, must be big enough to hold.

Sea shell: Talk about sizes, texture, where they come from, how they form.

Buy sea shell (different kinds and sizes) go to the beach and hide them.

Let the children look for them.

Magnifying glasses: Collect leaves, rocks, sticks, pine cones: Let children observe through magnifying glasses.

Nature walk: Have the children collect leaves, branches, pine cones and come back and do a collage at home.

Eggs and salt: Put salt into water, place eggs in water, see them float.

Pour fresh water in a container, place eggs see if they float.

Have a mystery bag with a variety of small objects: Have children guess what they are.

Collect baby food jars: Put some special water and a goldfish or snails with plant for feeding. Each child keeps a record of their fish or snail.

Go outside and feel the sidewalk with bare feet to see if it is hot or cold.

Make popsicles: Pour juice into ice cube containers. Talk about how it's watery now, but when it freezes it will become hard (popsicles).

Put chocolate pudding on a large flat container and let children play with it and eat it, especially toddlers.

CHAPTER XIII

SIMPLE CURRICULUM THEMES FOR EACH MONTH FOR YOU AND YOUR CHILD

Share this curriculum with your childcare provider if she does not have one. Go to your local library and find information about the theme for that certain month. For example for January, it's winter. You can check out books about snow, art activity book that demonstrates how to do winter activities with your child. Maybe take you child to the snow so that he/she can experience real snow.

JANUARY CURRICULUM
THEME: WINTER
GOALS:
1. Children will learn about different seasons
2. Children will learn about winter
3. Children will learn about snow
4. Children will learn about rain

ART ACTIVITIES
1. Make a snowman out of white construction paper. Have children cut circles and glue them on black construction paper.

2. Use popcorn for snowflakes. Show what happens to corn kernels when they are put in a pan to fry. Have children taste the popcorn and express their feelings.
3. Use ice cubes, place them in container so the children can touch and see how they melt.

ACTIVITIES
1. Warm clothing: Talk about jackets, gloves, hats and boots, sweaters; why we use them in the winter and not in the summer.
2. Snow: Study snow. Show large pictures of places where it snows: cities, mountains, country.
3. Field Trip: If possible, take children to the mountains where there is snow and let them explore.

FEBRUARY CIRRICULUM
THEME: HEALTH
GOALS:
1. Children will learn of good health habits.
2. Children will learn that eating the right foods makes us healthy.
3. Children will become aware that regular exercise and plenty of rest makes one healthy.
4. Children will learn that it is important to groom well.

ACTIVITIES:
1. Talk about body parts. Talk about the importance of body hygiene.
2. Vegetables Salad: Have children bring vegetables from home. Have them wash and cut vegetables. Discuss the importance of eating vegetables.
3. Daily Exercise: Put favorite albums on and have children exercise as a group, maybe one child leading the group with his favorite exercise.
4. Bath Dolls: Fill buckets of water. Add bubble bath and have children was dolls.

5. Carrot Cookies

   Write your recipe with pictographs

   1 Cup grated carrots

   1 Cup seedless raisins

   1 Cup flour

   ½ Cup honey or brown sugar

   2 tbsp. butter or margarine or vegetable oil

   Have the children grate carrots and mix with other ingredients. Bake at 350 degrees, bake for 20-30 minutes until cookies turn brown.

MARCH CIRRICULUM
THEME: WATER
GOALS:
1. Children will learn about different types of waters.
2. Children will learn that some fruits and vegetables contain water.
3. Children will learn about animals that live in water.
4. Children will learn that some things float while other do not
5. Children will learn how we get rain, hail, and snow.
6. Children will learn that our bodies need water in order to live.

ART ACTIVITIES:
1. Have children go through magazines and cut out fruits that contain water. Have them glue onto construction paper.
2. Get light-blue butcher paper. Post it on the wall, low enough so children can paint white clouds. Get dark blue paint to make rain drops.
3. Take children outside. Let them observe clouds: the colors, shapes, how they move and how rain takes place. Have children make clouds out of cotton balls glued to construction paper.

ACTIVITIES:
1. Floating Experience: Supply children with a large container filled with water. Get objects that float or sink. Have children predict it the object will float or sink.
2. Food Experience: Supply children with fruits that contain water or liquid and dry fruits. Explain the difference.
3. Wash Day: Have children wash the chairs and tables. Supply the children with sponges, rags and scrubbers, soap and water.

APRIL CIRRICULUM
THEME: GEOLOGY
GOALS:
1. Children will learn that the Earth is made up of water and land.
2. Children will learn that rivers, lakes and oceans all have different types of waters.
3. Children will learn how sand is formed.

ACTIVITIES:
1. Children stir and mix. Observe the change.
2. Salt water experience: Talk about ocean life. Have children cut sea animals from magazines and glue onto butcher paper. Have children glue sand on paper, giving it an ocean affect. Staple the mural on the wall.
3. Rocks: Discuss rocks: shapes, colors, textures, how they are formed. Collect rocks and paint them.
4. Drop Drill: Practice what to do during an earthquake. Explain about earthquakes.

MAY CIRRICULUM
THEME: NUTRITION/BASIC FOUR FOOD GROUPS
GOAL:
1. Children will learn the basic four food groups.
2. Children will learn that some foods come from plants and others from animals.

3. Children will learn that eating well balanced meals keeps your body healthy.
4. Children will learn that some foods could be eaten raw, that some have different flavors, and that some feel soft, hard, smooth, or rough.
5. Children will learn how to start a garden.

ACTIVITIES:
1. Carrot Raisin Man: Introduce carrots to children. Have children feel the carrots and talk about them (are they smooth? Are they short or long? Are they hairy, etc?). Have children talk about the color, taste, etc. Cut some carrots into small pieces and place on table- have children form a carrot man- supply some raisin for eyes. Have children eat their carrot man.
2. Green Fruits-Yellow Fruits: Introduce yellow and green vegetables and fruits. Talk about the fruits and vegetables (how they grow, where they grow, what color they are, and how they taste: sour or sweet?).
3. Butter: Use whipping cream, small jars, and yellow food coloring. Pour whipping cream into jars. Put lid on tightly. Have children shale until it becomes butter. Add a couple of drops of yellow food coloring. Have children enjoy the butter with saltine crackers.
4. Field Trip: Grocery in your neighborhood. Buy fruits and veggies, bring back and wash them. Enjoy them with sour cream.
5. Garden: Grow your own small garden. Carrots and beans are easy to grow, as well as pumpkins and squash.
6. Storytelling: Tell the children about a boy who ate veggies and fruits, drank milk, ate meats and breads and grew healthy, handsome, and strong. Stress how he developed strong bones and teeth, shiny hair, and nice complexion.

JUNE CIRRICULUM
THEME: CITY AND THE COUNTRY
GOALS:
1. Children will become aware that the city life is busy compared to the country life.
2. Children will learn that they city has more buildings.
3. Children will begin to realize that they life in the city is fast paced.

ART ACTIVITIES:
1. Using posters, books, and magazines, talk about the city. Extend learning on the different types of buildings, high rises, stores, streets, freeways, traffic, and people.
2. City Clothes: Have a child lay down on butcher paper. Trace the body and staple the sides together and stuff with paper. Cut out a tie, jacket, pants, etc. So that children can dress their paper person the way people dress in the city.
3. Country Clothes: Have a child lay down on butcher paper. Trace the child (remember make 2). Staple together. Cut out a shirt, overalls, boots and handkerchief so the children can dress their paper person like a farmer. Discuss the difference between country clothes and city clothes.
4. Display pictures of people working on the farm-talk about what they do and compare to city work.
5. Mural: have children cut out pictures from magazines that show people working out in the country. Have them glue on construction paper and post on wall like a mural.
6. Collages: Again cut out pictures that shows city life and country life out of magazines and glue on construction paper.

JULY CIRRICULUM
THEME: SUMMER FUN
GOALS:
1. Children will learn to swim.
2. Children will learn about signal lights.
3. Children will learn about trains.
4. Children will learn about watermelons, how they grow, what they taste like, how they feel.

ACTIVITES:
1. Enroll children in a swimming program.
2. Street Safety: Have children learn the signal lights. Cut out circles (green, red, yellow) and have children glue them on construction paper.
3. Field Trip: Take children to a car lot and talk about different transportations.
4. Take children to a train station and have them observe the train when they come in. Take children to a shed where trucks are being loaded with vegetables ready to be taken to the grocery store.
5. Watermelon Eating Contest: Cut watermelon pieces and place on table. Have children sit and time the children to see who eats the watermelon the fastest.

AUGUST CURRICULUM
THEME: TRANSPORTATION
GOALS:
1. Children will learn about different transportation methods.
2. They will be able to learn the names of different transportations.
3. Children will learn safety rules when crossing a street.

ART ACTIVITIES:
1. Collage: Have children cut out a variety of cars and trucks from magazines. Have then glue them on construction paper. Ask children about the picture- write what the children say.
2. Parachute: Make your own parachute out of an old king size sheet. Cut a round circle in the middle of the sheet to allow air flow. Place it will light balls, preferably balloons, nerf balls, or light rubber balls.
3. Explore Shells and Rocks: Take children to the beach. Collect shells and rocks. Bring them back to daycare and study them. What color are they? Does it feel smooth or rough? What shape are they? Do they smell? Paint the rocks different colors.

ACTIVITIES:
1. Counting Cars and Trucks: Have children go to front yard. Have them count all the cars and trucks in the neighborhood.
2. Picnic: Plan a picnic. Take a week to discuss what to take, how to act and how to follow rules when at the park. Play ball at the park.
3. Water Activity at Daycare: Buy a small swimming pool- fill it with only a couple of inches of water- let children sit in it and bathes dolls.

SEPTEMBER CURRICULUM
THEME: ENVIRONMENT
GOALS:
1. Children will become aware that the environment is composed of plants, animals, water, wind, birds, reptiles, etc.
2. Children will understand that the weather has an impact on the environment.
3. Children will learn of seasonal changes.

ART ACTIVITIES:
1. Animal collage
2. Plant collage
3. Make butterflies
4. Make bee hives
5. Make a bumble bee
6. Paint rocks and shells
7. Make kites
8. Make a farm and animals

ACTIVITIES
1. Talk about plants, animals, water, birds, reptiles, etc.
2. Take children to the beach, collect shells and rocks.
3. Take children to a zoo or museum.
4. Take children to library. Let them check out books about animals and plants.
5. Go out and catch butterflies, observe them and then let them go.

OCTOBER CURRICULUM
THEME: HALLOWEEN
GOALS:
1. The students learn of social events.
2. Students will learn symbols of Halloween.
3. Students will learn to follow safety rules.
4. Students will learn that Halloween is a time to have fun.

ART ACTIVITIES:
1. Pumpkin Experience: Have children learn about the pumpkin. Help them cut the pumpkin, take pulp out, feel it, talk about it, make a Jack-O-Lantern. For follow up activity, have children make their own pumpkin using modeling clay or play dough.

2. Paper Bag Pumpkin: Stuff paper bags with newspaper. Tie off top with rubber band. Have children paint them orange and glue on the features.
3. Spider Web: Draw a spider web on white construction paper, pour glue along lines and have children line with black yarn on glue. Draw favorite Halloween picture of bats, spiders, cats, etc., and glue them on the spider web.
4. Buy a big pumpkin- place it on a table. Make small holes so the children can place branches into the holes and paints so the children can paint whatever they feel like painting.

NOVEMBER CURRICULUM
THEME: HARVEST
GOALS:
1. Children will learn the difference between fruits and vegetables.
2. Children will learn that some foods need to be cooked before eaten. Also, they will learn that some vegetables can be eaten raw.
3. Children will learn about "Harvesting". What it means and time of celebration in various cultures around the world.
4. Children will learn about potato plants. How to plant them, how to care for them.

ACTIVITIES:
1. Potato Plant: Put a little dirt in the bottom of the cup. Drop the potato chunk into the cup. Cover will more dirt. Water well. Have children plant their own potato chunk. After, place the cups on the science center shelf to grow. Have each child clean up his own area.
2. Ben collage: Demonstrate how to make a bean collage with assortment of beans (including fresh ones). Distribute the paper and glue. Then let the children make a wild and wonderful bean collage with the piles of beans.

3. Horn of Plenty: Hold up picture of Horn-of-Plenty. Ask "What do you suppose this is?" This is called a horn of plenty and it is usually a sign of a good harvest. Around this time of year, you might see a horn of plenty picture in the grocery store. This is their way of showing the harvest was good this year.

DECEMBER CURRICULUM
THEME: CHRISTMAS
GOALS:
1. Children will learn of the social events.
2. Children will learn that Christmas is a time to give and greet others.
3. Children will learn to understand that Christmas is a holiday season.
4. Children will become aware that Christmas is celebrated around the world.

ACTIVITIES:
1. Christmas Tree: Have children cut two identical shapes of a Christmas tree from poster board. In one, make a slit in the middle from top to the center, and in the other slit should be from bottom to the center of the trunk. Have children pass one from bottom to the center of the trunk. Have children pass one over through the slit. Glue them together to keep them in place. Have children fix it on a wooden or clay base. Have the children decorate the tree with sequins, stars, glitters, etc.
2. Christmas Wreath: Using collage materials: paper plates, macaroni, buttons, pine cones, old ribbons, bows, olive leaves, or any other material of your choice, glue or paste to a rime of a thick paper plate. When gluing make sure the children arrange them to get the appearance of a wreath. When dry, spray silver or gold paint (optional).

3. Christmas Stockings: Place together two old Christmas cards of same size, blank side inward. Cut the shape of a stocking and punch holes using a hole puncher. Have children pass a string or yarn lacing the stockings.
4. Bells: (From Styrofoam cups) Using small cups (yogurt, ice cream, water, Styrofoam) have children glue tissue papers to cover surface. Make a hole on the bottom, pass a string through, and hang on the tree.
5. Chains: Use different shape macaroni. Dye them with food coloring and have the children string them together to make long chains. Join together and use to decorate the tree.
6. Storytelling: Go to the library check out books on how Christmas is celebrated around the world.
7. Christmas Dinner: Set up a table. Decorate with crafts that they children made. Let children choose what they want to eat. Set up the table family style. Let children serve themselves and pass bowl around the table, giving the children the opportunity to choose what they want to eat. Encourage children to try a little bit of everything.
8. Get some black construction paper. Place white paint on the table and let children paint snow on the black construction paper. If they can, have them draw a house and tree and snow coming down.

MY FAVORITE SONGS / POEMS

The following songs can be sung or learned as poems. These songs are favorites to everyone. Share with your childcare provider. They are familiar because they are old Nursery Rhymes.

Twinkle, Twinkle, Little Star

Twinkle, twinkle, little star,
How I wonder what you are!
Up above the world so high,
Like a diamond in the sky.

Here We Go Round

Here we go round the mulberry bush,
The mulberry bush, the mulberry bush,
Here we go round the mulberry bush,
So early in the morning.

Ring Around The Rosies

Ring around the rosies
A pocket full of posies
Hush! Hush! Hush!
All fall down.

London Bridge

London Bridge, is falling down,
Falling down, falling down,
London Bridge is falling down
My fair lady.
Build it up with wood and clay,
Wood and clay, wood and clay,

Build it up with wood and clay,
My fair lady.

Where Has My Little Dog Gone?

Oh, where, Oh where,
Has my little dog gone?
Oh, where, Oh where can he be
With his ears cut short
And his tail cut long.
Oh where, Oh where, can he be?

I Send a Letter To My Love

I sent a letter to my love,
And on the way I dropped it,
A little puppy picked it up
And put it in his pocket

Hickory Dickory Dock

Hickory dickory dock
The mouse ran up the clock!
The clock struck one
And down he ran,
Hickory, dickory, dock.

Yankee Doodle

Yankee doodle went to town
Riding on a pony,
Struck a feather in his hat
And called it macaroni.

The Muffin Man

Oh, do you know the muffin man,
The muffin man, the muffin man,
Oh, do you know the muffin man
Who lives in Drury Lane?
Oh yes, I know the muffin man,
The muffin man, the muffin man,
Oh yes, I know the muffin man
Who lives in Drury Lane.

Jack and Jill

Jack and Jill went up the hill
To fetch a pail of water,
Jack fell down
And broke his crown
And Jill came tumbling after.

Mary Had A Little Lamb

Mary had a little lamb
It's fleece was white as snow.
And everywhere that Mary went
The lamb was sure togo.

Hush-A Bye Baby

Hush-a-bye, baby
On the tree top
When the wind blows
The cradle will rock.
When the bough bends
The cradle will fall
And down will come baby
Cradle and all

One Two Buckle My Shoe

One, two, buckle my shoe
Three, four, shut the door
Five, six pick up sticks
Seven, eight, lay them straight
Nine, ten, big fat hen

How Many Days

How many days has my baby
to play?
Saturday, Sunday, Monday,
Tuesday, Wednesday,
Thursday, Friday,
Saturday, Sunday, Monday.

This Old Man

This old man, he played one
He played knick knack on his thumb
Knick knack paddy whack, give your dog a bone
This old man came rolling home.
This old man, he played two
He played knick knack on his shoe
Knick knack, paddy whack, give your dog a bone
This old man came rolling home.
This old man, he played three
He played knick knack on his knee.
Knick, knack paddy whack, give your dog a bone
This old man came rolling home.
This old man, he played four
He played knick knack on the floor
Knick knack, paddy whack, give your dog a bone
This old man came rolling home.

This old man, he played five
He played knick, knack on the drive
Knick, knack paddy whack, give your dog a bone
This old man came rolling home.

Clap Your Hands

If you're happy and you know it
Clap your hands, (clap, clap)
If you're happy and you know it
Clap your hands, (clap, clap)
If your happy and you know it
Then your face will surely show it
If you're happy and you know it
Clap your hands, (clap, clap)
Repeat with stamp your feet
Repeat with turn around, etc.

Where Is Thumbkin

(Use your fingers)
[Start with both hands behind back]
Where is Thumbkin? Where is Thumbkin?
Here I am. Here I am.
How are you today, sir?
Very well, thank you.
Run away, run away.
[Repeat with Pointer, Tallman, Ringman, and Pinkie.

Teddy Bear

Teddy bear, teddy bear
Touch the ground.
Teddy bear, teddy bear
Turn around.

Teddy bear, teddy bear
Tie your shoe.
Teddy bear, teddy bear
That will do.
Teddy bear, teddy bear
Go upstairs.
Teddy bear, teddy bear
Say your prayers.
Teddy bear, teddy bear
Turn out the light.
Teddy bear, teddy bear
Say "Goodnight".

Where Is Susie

Where, oh where, is little dear Susie?
Where, oh where, is little dear Susie?
Where, oh where, is little dear Susie?
Way down yonder in the paw-paw patch.
Picking up paw-paws, put'em in a basket.
Picking up paw-paws, put'em in a basket.
Picking up paw-paws, put'em in a basket.
Way down yonder in the paw-paw patch.
Well come on children, let's go get her
Well come on children, let's go get her
Well come on children, let's go get her
Way down yonder in the paw-paw patch.

The Itsy Bitsy Spider

The Itsy Bitsy spider went up the water spout.
Down came the rain and washed the spider out.
Out came the sun and dried up all the rain.
And the Itsy Bitsy spider went up the spout again.

Who Took The Cookies From The Cookie Jar?

___child___ took the cookies from the cookie jar.
___child___: Who me?
___all___: Yes, you!
___child___: Couldn't be.
___all___: then who?
___2nd child___ took the cookies from the cookie jar.
___2nd child___: Who me?
___all___: Yes, you!
Repeat for each child as above.

Teapot

I'm a little teapot short and stout.
Here is my handle,
Here is my spout.
When I get all steamed up then I shout
Just tip me over and pour me out.

Hush, Little Baby

Hush little baby don't say a word
Mama's going to but you a mocking bird.
If that mocking bird don't sing
Mama's going to buy you a diamond ring.
If that diamond ring turn brass
Mama's going to buy you a looking glass.
If the looking glass gets broke
Mama's going to buy you a billy goat.
If that billy goat won't pull
Mama's going to buy you a cart and bull.
If that cart and bull turn over
Mama's going to buy you a dog named Rover.
If that dog named Rover won't bark

Mama's going to buy you a horse and cart.
If the horse and cart fall down
You'll still be the prettiest girl in town.

Georgie Porgie

Georgie Porgie,
Pudding and pie,
Kissed that girls
And made them cry.
When the boys
Came out to play,
Georgie Porgie ran away.

Little Jumping Joan

Here am I,
Little jumping Joan.
When nobody's with me
I'm always alone.

Jack Be Nimble

Jack, be nimble
Jack, be quick
Jack, jump over
The candle stick.

Pease-Porridge Hot

Pease-porridge hot,
Pease-porridge cold
Pease-porridge in the pot,
Nine days old
Some like it hot,

Some like it cold
Some like it in the pot,
Nine days old.

Humpty Dumpty

Humpty Dumpty sat on a wall,
Humpty Dumpty had a great fall.
All the king's horses
And all the king's men
Couldn't put Humpty together again.

Hey Diddle Diddle

Hey! Diddle, diddle!
The cat and the fiddle,
The cow jumped over the moon.
The little dog laughed
To see such sport,
And the dish ran away with the spoon.

There Was a Crooked Man

There was a crooked man
Who walked a crooked mile
He found a crooked sixpence
Against a crooked stile.
He bought a crooked cat,
Which caught a crooked mouse,
And they all lived together
In a little crooked house.

I Had Two Birdies

I had two birdies bright and gay,
They flew from me the other day,
What was the reason they did go?
I cannot tell for I do not know.

Mary, Mary Quite Contrary

Mary, Mary quite contrary, how does your garden grow?
With silver bells
And cockleshells,
And pretty maids all in a row.

Peter, Peter, Pumpkin-Eater

Peter, Peter, pumpkin-eater
Had a wife and couldn't keep her.
He put her in a pumpkin shell
And there he kept her very well.

A Diller, A Dollar

A diller, a dollar,
A ten o'clock scholar,
What makes you come so soon?
You used to come at ten o'clock.
And now you come and noon.

Pat-A-Cake

Pat-a-cake, pat-a-cake,
Bakers man.
Bake me a cake
As fast as you can.

Pat it and prick it,
And mark it with a B,
And put it in the oven for baby and me.

There Was An Old Woman Lived Under A Hill

There was an old woman
Lived under a hill,
And if she's not gone
She lives there still.

Little Bo Peep

Little Bo Peep has lost her sheep
And can't tell where to find them,
Leave them alone,
And they'll come home,
Wagging their tales behind them.

Dickery, Dickery, Dare

Dickery, dickery, dare,
The pig flew up in the air.
The man in brown
Soon brought him down,
Dickery, dickery, dare.

I'm Glad The Sky Is Painted Blue

I'm glad the sky is painted blue,
And earth is painted green,
With such a lot of nice fresh air
All sandwiched in between.

Two Little Blackbirds

Two little blackbirds
Sitting on a hill
One named Jack,
The other named Jill,
Fly away, Jack,
Fly away, Jill.
Come back, Jack,
Come back, Jill.

CHAPTER XIV

MY FAVORITE CHILDREN BOOKS

Be My Valentine, Charlie Brown: By Charles M. Schulz

Love Is a Special Way of Feeling: By Joan Walsh Anglund

Be my Valentine,: By Miriam Cohen

The Growing Tree: ?

The Three Billy Goats Gruff: By Peter Christian Asbjornsen

Where the Wild Things Are: By Maurice Sendak

The House That Jack Built: By Paul Galdone

The Little Red Hen: By Paul Galdone

Brown Bear, Brown Bear What Do You See?: By Bill Martin Jr.

Silly Goose: By Omerod

I Can't Said the Ant: Polly Cameron

I Hate to Take a Bath: By Judi Barrett

Anabelle Swift, Kindergartner: By Schwartq

Bathtime: By Jean Bethell

The Strawberry Book of Colors: By Richard Heffer

Adventures of Three Colors: By Annette Tison and Talus Taylor

In the Rain: By Anne Rockwell

It Looked Like Split Milk: By Charles Shaw

Hello Cloudes!: By Dalia Renberg

All Fall Down: By Helen Oxenbury

Growing: By Fiona Pragoff

Biggest Snowstorm Ever: By Diane Patersn

Josie and the Snow: By Helen Buckley

Why You Feel Hot, Why You Feel Cold: Your Body Temperature: By James Barry

Pete's Pup, Kathy's Kitty: By Syd Holt

What Do You Do With a Kangaroo?: By Mercer Mayer

The Bear's Toothache: By David McPhail

Old McDonald Had a Farm: By Moritz Kennel

The Farmer in the Dell: By mary Maki Rae

Oh What a Mess!: By Wilhelm

Corduroy: By Don Freeman

Boy with a Problem: By Joan Fassler

Stone Soup: By Marcia Brown

Bears on Wheels: By Stan and Jan Berenstain

Is It Red? Is It Yellow? Is It Blue?: By Tana Hoban

One Fish, Two Fish, Red Fish, Blue Fish: By Dr. Seuss

Alexander and the Terrible, Horrible, No Good, Very Bad Day:?

Naughty Nancy: By John Gooddall

Know Your Fruits, Know Your Vegetables: Jules Books

Pet Store: By Peter Spier

Is It Larger, Is It Smaller?: By Tana Hoban

My Five Senses: By Aliki

Good Night Moon: By Brown

The Little Engine That Could: By Piper

Thump-Thump Rat-a-Tat-Tat: By Gene Baer

Baby Bear's Bedtime Book: By Jane Yolen

I Read Signs: By Tana Hoban.

Book of Nursery and Mother Goose Rhymes: By marguerite DeAngeli

Animals on the Farm: By Feodor Rojankovsky

Chicken Little: By Steven Kellogg

Curious George: By Hans Augusto Rey

Rain Makes Applesauce: By Julian Scheer

The Cat in the Hat: By Dr. Seuss

Little Toot: By Hardie Gramatky

I am Going On a Bear Hunt: By Sandra Stroner Sivulich

Caps for Sale: Esphyr Slobodkina

Make Way for Ducklings: By McCloskey

Ask Mr. Bear: By Marjorie Flack

Are You My Mommy?: By Philip D. Eastman

Green Eggs and Ham: By Dr. Seuess

Tortillas Para Mama: By Margo Griego

Popcorn: By Frank Asch

Put Me In The Zoo: By Robert Lopshire

The Rainbow: By Mike Thaler

CHAPTER XV

ACTIVITIES FOR YOUR INFANT

Exercise the infant---massage the infant.

Talk to the infant throughout the day.

Carry the infant—take the infant out for fresh air.

Move infant around but keep him where they can be observed.

Sit with infant on carpet and roll toys to him.

Put infant on stomach so that he can develop muscles.

Place toys in front of infant so that he can try to reach them.

Put child in front of a mirror so that he can see himself.

Take infant outside and place him in a sandbox barefoot.

Chocolate pudding-place eating tray by infant, and let infant experiment with it.

Make fruit jello—let infant experiment with it.

Sing to the child—you will be surprised how they learn to memorize the sounds. Quick.

Let infant be barefoot and walk on different textures.

Read to infant—they are never too young to be read to. Mothers are reading to babies when the baby is still in the womb.

Play peek-a-boo with infant. Use blankets, hide behind furniture, hide behind other children.

Put music on and hold baby, softly dance with him.

Put instrumental music on when baby is asleep.

Place large ice cubes in a bowl. Let infants experiment with it.

Blow bubbles for the infants—let them observe them.

Take infants for a ride on a wagon or stroller around the neighborhood.

Let infant experience with mud.

Make noodles and spaghetti; let infant experience with them.

Place paint on butcher paper and let infants touch and make designs with their hands.

Fill up a small bucket with water and let infant splash the water, causing him to get wet.

Lay infant on his back and raise legs up and down and bent them also.

Always remember your infant is fragile and they can easily be hurt. Be gentle and caring toward their needs and you will develop a happy human being. A person that will be successful throughout his life, no matter what he encounters. As a professional in child development my main concern is that the child be treated with love and dignity.

The rest of the learning process will come automatically.

The recipe that follows is my own creation. It's simple and easy to make.

I used it a lot during my years as a child care provider. Children love to play with it because it is easy to knead and cut using cookie cutters. The children will spend hours of making their own creations.

PLAY DOUGH RECIPE:

Flour—As much as you want, usually half a bowl or 8 cup

Oil ½ cup

Water: Start out with a cup of water, then keep adding water using your own discrepancy

until it becomes dough. You don't want it sticky and runny. You want it to be like cookie dough, easy to roll and knead. Easy for the children to be able to roll it into a ball or spread it like a pie crust.

Optional: You can add food coloring or leave it plain. I recommend leaving it plain

just because the food coloring will stain your carpet.

Food coloring-add food coloring to water before pouring it into the flour ingredients.

Mix all ingredients together creating a big ball of dough.

Store in container with a tight lid. Store in refrigerator.

CHAPTER XVI

CHILD CARE HOME PROGRAMS OBSERVATIONS

OBSERVATION I

The setting in this house is excellent. The house has a lot of room for the children to play in. Her living room is large. She has removed her coffee table so the living room is quite large to play in. The garage is converted into a play room. It is excellent, has a lot of toys for the children. The children look very happy, they are treated like family. They are allowed to sit on the chairs in the living room The husband is her helper. When I arrived he was holding an infant and bottle feeding him. The rest of the children were having breakfast in the dining room. Just like if they were part of the family. While talking with me, the home provider picked up an infant and rocked him to sleep. I thought that was great. She gave the infant personal attention for a while. The back yard has a wall fenced all around. The wall is about twelve feet high. The neighbors cannot see over the fence nor are able to jump over. Children are allowed to see Barney after they finish eating. The home provider changed a diaper while her husband cleans the kitchen and play area.

The home provider allows children to come to her program in their pajamas. She dresses them later, which I thought was great for the working parents. The atmosphere is very pleasant. The husband seems to enjoy working with children. They have two children of their own, so this type of business is a great way to spend time with their children plus make money. They are very clean, she cleans the infant's nose pretty regular. Children were allowed to watch two educational videos after they are finished with their breakfast. After the videos they were all led to the play area, which is the garage. They had free play.

At 11:30 a.m. they had lunch. They had a nutritional meal: Quesadilla, chicken soup with vegetables, fruit and milk. After lunch they went outside to play. Nap time is 1:00-3:00p.m. Both providers use soft voices toward the children. The children show a lot of love toward both of the providers. The providers are attending college. Both are taking early childhood classes.

OBSERVATION II

As I arrived the children were finishing breakfast. Childcare is held in the living room. The provider and assistant wear aprons with their nicknames on them and the business name, which I thought it was very clever. There is 7 children present. 2 infants and 5 toddlers.

The provider sits on the floor and interacts with the children. The provider is getting ready for a Christmas Party. The party will start at 5:30p.m. The provider made dozens of tamales to share with her parents. She does this event every year for parents and the children. Santa Claus will be here around 6:oop.m. She takes pictures of the children with Santa and gives them to the parents. I thought that was very nice of her to go out of her way to make this gathering during the holidays for her parents. I feel by doing this, the provider and parents maintain a closeness throughout the year. The children call the provider "Nana", which I thought was a beautiful way to relate with the children. "Nana" in English means grandmother. The children relate with their caretaker as their grandmother, making their relationship genuine. I thought that was why home childcare is healthy for children because they are allowed to call their caretaker their own special name, creating a closeness between the provider and the children. The provider has two sons, one 14 and the other 15. Both help to care, they play baseball, football, jump rope, etc.

As children finish eating their lunch they are trained to take their plate and cup to the sink. I thought that was a great way to teach responsibility. Children are allowed to play with blocks, legos, and puzzles for half and hour. The children are put down to nap around 12:30p.m. The provider uses all her bedrooms during nap time. Each child has their own blanket and mat. For lunch the children had hot nutritional meal. They had hamburger meat with macaroni, green salad, bananas, milk and wheat bread. The provider is attending college. She is taking early child development classes.

OBSERVATION III

When I arrived the provider was feeding the children breakfast. She served scrambled eggs, wheat flour tortillas, milk and oranges. The childcare was very immaculate. The entire house looks very clean and smells clean. The garage is attached to the house and is converted into an activity area. The floor has linoleum. The shelves are painted bright red, yellow and white. The colors are very attractive to children. The provider has a variety of videos (Walt Disney) for the children. She also has many toys and games that the children are allowed to play with. She interacts with the children very well. The children look very content and happy. Lunch menu is macaroni and cheese, salad, milk and apples. She worries when the children do not eat. She makes sure all the children try each food. The provider's childcare is very attractive and inviting to the children. I thought the bright colors she uses in the activity area is excellent. The back yard is fenced and has a lot of space where children can play. She has a variety of outdoor equipment (Little Tykes). The provider's nieces are helping her with the children. They feed the infants, change diapers and play with them. They also cook breakfast, which I thought that was excellent. Children lay down to take a nap around 12:30p.m.-3:00p.m. The children are able to lay down in the bedrooms. The provider earned her CDA Certificate (Child Development Associate)

OBSERVATION IV

I arrived at 10:00. The provider is watering the plants outside. There is 6 children present. The children are playing in the sandbox, and climbing equipment. The children looked very happy. They said hi and continued playing. The provider offered a variety of playing areas. She has a water table with tiny toys, sandbox full of sand, a claiming gym that had a big slide, a bicycle area, and basketball area. Her patio is covered, which is an excellent idea because the summers are very hot. Children went in to use bathroom and wash their hands, Children got ready for lunch. Lunch menu is taco with cheese and lettuce and tomatoes, canned peaches, and milk. The children ate for 45 minutes. Play Time outside. Children again played on the claiming equipment for 30 minutes. Children came in and used bathroom and washed hands. Children got ready for nap time. Each child had a mat and blanket .Children removed their shoes. Children slept for 21/2 hrs. The garage was converted into an activity room. It has heating and air conditioning, which is nice for the children. The provider has a daughter that arrived from high school. She helps her with the children once they wake up and are ready to play outdoors.

She plays with the children kick ball outside.

OBSERVATION V

I arrived at 9:00am. Children present is 2 infants 5 toddlers and 3 year old. The provider was cleaning the table. She uses the living room and formal dining area as part of the childcare. The children are doing art activity. They are cutting shapes. The children call the provider "mom". The children are bonded with the family. They smile and look happy.

The house has an extra room where children sleep. Each child has a blanket and mat. Their names are posted on the wall. The child knows where to place the mat. Each child has a cubby for their belongings. They place art activities inside the cubby. In the living room are cribs for the infants. Her mother takes care of the infants and the provider takes care of the toddlers, and 3 to 4 year old while they nap. Children remove their shoes right before nap time. Her husband is cleaning the kitchen. The childcare program has a preschool program. The children have snack at 3:00pm. Snack is crackers and cheese and juice. After snack children went out to play. Mother lives with her.

OBSERVATION VI

I arrived at 9:00am. 7 children were present: 2 infants and 5 toddlers. The provider was feeding the children. It was the end of the breakfast routine. Children ate cereal, milk, and a banana. Children played indoor until 9:45 am. The provider place legos on one table and place puzzles on another table for the children to play with. Children went out to play at 9:45. The provider has a beautiful backyard. She has half of her backyard covered. Great idea for the summer sun and rainy days. She has a big ball hanging and the children love to hit and kick the ball.. Children are having fun. Provider has a large play gym, and a dramatic play area where the children can slide down and land in the dramatic area. Clever idea. Children go in and use restroom and wash hands. Children get ready for lunch. Menu is chicken stew, green salad, orange slices, milk. Children are socializing among themselves. The assistant helps cook clean and sometimes play outside with the children. The children get ready for nap time. They remove their shoes. They sleep for 2 hours. Her mother helps her by reading stories to the children. The provider has earned her AA in child development. She is the President of the association for home childcare providers.

OBSERVATION VII

Arrived at 9:30a.m. The provider greeted me at the door with a little one in her arms. There is 8 children present: 2 infants and 6 toddlers. The provider had a back room added to her house. She also had a kitchen build just for the program. She does not enter her home at all. There is a side door where parents can drop off their child. The provider cooks in the kitchen while her son helps with the children. The son reads a story and sings songs with the children. They practice the colors and ABC'S. The son takes the children outside while mom finishes lunch. The back yard is great. She has it covered with a net. She has an area where children ride bikes. Her husband painted arrows going one way and the children follow directions. She has a play gym, and a play house. The children are having fun.

The children went in and washed their hands and used the bathroom. The provider changed the diapers. Children went to sit at the table and waited for the provider to put food on the table. The provider serves family style meals. The children served themselves. I thought that was excellent to see the children serve themselves and at the same time socializing with their friends. The children ate for 45 minutes and then went out to play for 30 minutes before they had to lay down for a nap. The provider has her AA in child development.

OBSERVATION VIII

Arrived at 10:30. There are 6 children present, 2 infant and 4 toddlers.

The provider had the garage converted into an activity area.. She had a table, a couple of cribs, dramatic play area with lots of dolls, cooking appliances, science area, and a book area where the children can reach a book and lay on a mat to read and relax. Children were doing an art activity. They were making a snowman. After finishing their art project they were given permission to go outside to play.

The helper played with the children kick ball. The provider stayed with the infants in door. Provider changed diapers and fed the infants.

Children went in around 11:30 a.m. They washed their hands and used the restroom. Children were ready for lunch. Lunch was served at 12:00. Lunch menu:

Soft tacos, lettuce and tomatoes, cheese, oranges and milk. Well balanced meal. Children ate for 40 minutes. Children went out to play for 20 minutes. The children came in used the restroom and washed hands. Mats were put down and each mat had a blanket. Children removed their shoes. Children giggled as they took off their shoes. Children feel comfortable. Children slept 21/2 hours. Instrumental music was turned on while children slept. Children went straight to sleep. The provider has earned her AA in child development. Her daughter helps her. The daughter has her preschool Permit.

OBSERVATION IX

Arrived at 9:00a.m. 8 children present. 2 infants and 6 toddlers. The childcare provider was very professional. She greeted me and took me into her childcare area.

The garage was converted into a play area. Another extra small room was designed for infants. The back yard was appropriately equipped. A large area outside was covered with canvas, which I thought it was excellent due to the summer sun. Children seem to be happy playing with a variety of toys. Children call the provider

"mom" which I thought the children were bonded with her. Children go inside at 10:30 and used the restroom and washed hands. Children play inside for 40 minutes. Children again wash hands and use restroom and got ready for lunch.

Lunch menu is noodles with hamburger meat, bread, apple slices, and milk.

Children ate lunch for 45 minutes. Her daughter helps her with the children. Daughter attends college in the evening. Children went out to play for 45 minutes.

Children come in and use restroom and wash hands. Children get ready for nap.

Children remove their shoes. Children sleep for 2 1/2 hours. Provider has her CDA (Child Development Associate Degree). Provider wants to continue her education in child development. Provider is the secretary of the association for home childcare providers.

OBSERVATION X

Arrived at 9:00

The provider greeted me at the door. She led me to the childcare area. Her husband build her a room for childcare. It's beautiful. She has an area for infants and toddlers. She is always full. She has a waiting list of parents that want to get enrolled into her program. She has tables where children eat lunch. There is a gate between kitchen and childcare area. She has a helper that helps her with the children and another that picks up children from school. The program has 14 children. Outdoors she has another dramatic play area. She has a lot of toys in the dramatic area. There are a lot of toys for the children to pull, ride, and push.

Lunch was chicken and veggie stew, bananas, milk, bread. Children seem content.

Children come in and use restroom and wash hands and get ready to have lunch.

She has a daily schedule posted where parents can see what's going on as they walk in. Children eat for 45 mins., than they go outside and play for 30 mins. Children come in and use restroom wash hands and lay down and take a nap. Nap is 12:30 to 3:00pm. Children take shoes off whiling napping. Every child has a matt and blanket. No music is put on she said children hear the music and start to dance, instead of napping. She and her helper go around and tap the children back until they fall asleep. The provider is attending college. She has two years of college.

She is studying toward a B.A. in child development.

CHAPTER XVIII

CHILD DEVELOPMENT CENTERS OBSERVATIONS

OBSERVATION I

The childcare center was located in the neighborhood. It was a house converted into a childcare center. Arrive at 8:00am. The house has three bedrooms. The center has 24 children. She has an assistant. The assistant has college units. She qualifies as an associate teacher. The director which is the teacher also, has her B,A. in child development.

The preschoolers are doing an art activity. It was winter so they were making snowmen. They discussed winter and how cold it is. Children talk about wearing jackets to school. After activity they get ready to go outside to play. They play kick ball with the assistant. The teacher stays indoors with the infants. Each baby is held by the teacher and fed. The children played for 40 mins. They come in use the restroom and wash hands. The children get ready to eat lunch. Children eat lunch and socialize with friends for 40 mins. Lunch menu is chicken soup, wheat bread, apple slices, milk. Children are given permission to play for 30 mins. before napping. Children come in and use restrooms and wash hands.

A mat and blanket are placed on the floor. Children know the routine. Children sleep for 21/2 hrs. Children wake up at 3:00pm. It is snack time. They have yogurt and pineapple bits Children finish snack than are able to go out doors to play. The children had free play. Parents start to arrive to pick up their children.

OBSERVATION II

Childcare center is a house and located in a nice neighborhood. Arrived at 8:00am. They have an infant program. The teacher moves the infants around. They have three infants. Each infant has a crib. The program has a diaper changing area. The infants are monitored and recorded every time they ate, bowel movement, urinated, or had an unusual incident. The staff moved around so the infants had a new caretaker every 4 hrs. Due to lack of staff the infant program was not having quality time with the infants. The infants were held when being fed. The caretaker sits on a rocking chair and feeds the infant. After feeding the infant is place back in the crib.

OBSERVATION III

Arrived at 8:00a.m. The children are having breakfast. They are having boiled eggs, English muffin, milk, and apple. The children are peeling their boiled eggs.

They seem to be enjoying the experience. Each child put his/her plate in the trash after finishing their breakfast. Each child took a paper towel and cleaned their area.

Teacher gives directions to the children to go to activity tables. Children choose the table they want to go to. The center is very structured. It looks like a kindergarten class. The children are busy doing activities. Children must finish their activities quick. Teacher tells the children to finish and is constantly repeating it. The children look like robots, they do not look relaxed. The children do not look happy in this type of learning environment. Not once did the children ask questions or socialize among themselves or call the teacher by her name. They were not encouraged to express their feelings or ask questions. I feel I am in an empty class. There is no excitement among the children. These are pre-school children

OBSERVATION IV

Arrived at 8:00 am. Children are having breakfast. They look happy and content.

Breakfast menu is cereal, milk, and fruit. There is one teacher to every table.

There are four tables and eight children per table. After children finished breakfast

They picked up their plate, spoon, fork, and cup and placed them in a large container. Each child gets a clean white towel and clears his/her area. After child finishes cleaning their area he/she goes to use bathroom and washes hands. Each child has their own toothbrush. They brush teeth, rinse and go sit down on the carpet. It is circle time. Teacher goes through the weather, days of the week, name of the months, ABC'S, colors, numbers. After circle time children go to activity tables. They have a choice of activity table. Children must go to every activity table before they are allowed to go out to play. Children put their jackets and line up at the door. Names are called out. Every child answers. Teachers put a variety of activities outside. Children have choices where they want to go first.

OBSERVATION V

Infant/Toddler Program

Arrived at 8:00am. The center had 3 infants and 9 toddlers. The ratio was excellent.

The center is located in a labor camp. The program is federally funded. It serves migrant workers that come in from Arizona, Texas, and Utah to harvest the grapes. Each child has his/her crib. The cribs are separate from the toddlers. The infant program one teacher and one assistant for every 3 infants. Excellent teacher/Infant ratio. The teacher records when the child feeds, and has a diaper change. They also record an assessment of each child as they progress in their development. The infant is never left alone. The teacher and assistant take turns watching them. The teacher and assistant are educated in early child development. Some have degrees in early child development. The room looks like a childcare but it lacks the home environment that is healthy for the infants and toddlers.

OBSERVATION VI

Infant Program. I arrived at 9:00am. There is 4 infants and 6 toddlers. The ratio is one teacher for every 4 infants. Diapers are changed regular. Area is large and carpeted where older infants are allowed to play. The teacher say it's 90% play and 10% sleep. One year and younger must furnish their own baby food, diapers, and wipes. There is plenty of toys. The center is set up like a learning center. Two tables, one diaper changer, and sink. The teacher uses computer paper to put under the child while he/she is being changed. Sunday school uses the center on weekend. They lock everything up on Friday so that no one can use their materials. Teacher said they use to have a sofa but that teachers use to sit on it and would not interact with the children. Parents bring blankets from home. Blankets send home on Friday to be washed. Menu is peanut butter and jam sandwiches, cheese, carrot sticks, and apple slices. The fifteen month and older were able to eat what is on the menu. Teacher cleans the table while older infants played. After playing awhile teacher starts changing diapers and removing shoes and socks. The children nap for 21/2 hours. They nap at different times. Snack at 3:00pm. Cookies and juice. Children play until parents start to arrive. The center was too structured. It looked like a classroom and not like a home setting.

OBSERVATION VII

Arrived at 8:30am. Children playing outside. The program participates on the Foster Grandparent Program. Two grandparents were outside playing with the children. The children call them grandma and grandpa. The children look happy and relate to them very well. The ratio is five adults and 24 children. The center is at a church. They have classrooms and looks like a school. The center has enough shade for the children. They do not participate in the Food program, so the children bring their own lunch. The program offers morning snack and afternoon snack. Lunch is at 12:00. Children go outside to play for approximately 20 minutes.

Children come in and use restroom and wash hands. Naptime at 12:45 to 3:00pm.

At 3:00 they have snack and go outside to play until parents arrive. The center was structured like a classroom and not like a home setting environment, which I feel it's healthier for children that are in childcare all day.

OBSERVATION VIII

Arrived at 8:00am. Funded program. Center located in a church. There are 75 children. The church has classrooms. The teachers and children speak Spanish. They have one room strictly for dramatic play All classrooms share the dramatic play at different times. The carpet is worn out. Tape is used to cover the torn edges. The carpet smells old and dirty. The classrooms were very colorful. All materials are in Spanish and English. The building is very old, which makes the program look run down. Outside play was well equipped. Lunch menu was frozen meals.

I thought it was not appropriate for the children. The program is 100% Hispanic descent. Complaint from the children that the food was not warm enough. For snack they have cookies and juice every day. They participate in the Senior Program and Youth Program. The program place seniors and youth at the center to help out. The center is setup like a school. It has classrooms. The center did not look to inviting to the younger group. The younger groups had to go out of the classroom to be able to use the restroom. An adult would accompany them. The church would let their congregation go in to the center and do what they had to do. I feel that is impropriate while the center is operating.

OBSERVATION IX

Arrived 8:30 a.m. Introduce myself to with site supervisor. Center is funded by the Richgrove school district. All children are of Hispanic descent. Richgrove is a small farmworkers town. There is one teacher and one assistant with 24 children. The center is quite small. It had a science center, which is very attractive to the children.

Children look happy but not much conversation was going on. Children are told what to do, there is no choice of activities for them. Children went out to play after the activity was done. Outdoor play area is small. No shade for the children. Children played for ½ hour. Children came in used the restroom and washed their hands. Children ate cafeteria food just like the school age children. Children are put down to nap right after lunch. Children slept for 2 hours. Parents started to arrive at 3:00p.m. I think the center is quite small for 24 children. The center is setup like a classroom. Children cannot enjoy themselves inside because everything is put in place and has no space for children to play. They practice structured play inside.

OBSERVATION X

I arrived at 8:00 am. The center is located in a housing authority camp. The center is a large building divided into learning centers. The toddler program was away from the preschoolers. The room is set up like a kindergarten classroom. There is eight toddlers and two adults. One is a teacher and the other associate teacher.

The children are eating their breakfast. Cereal, pears and milk. During breakfast the toddlers ate together. They did not make any noise while they ate. The toddlers were taken outside each holding a rope. One teacher was in the back and the other in the front leading the toddlers out. There is plenty of toys for the toddlers. The toddlers had a water table and a play house. Toddlers come in and out of the play house. Toddlers played for 30 minutes outside. The toddlers are brought in and have their diapers change and wash hands. Toddlers played inside with blocks neasel painting . Toddlers get ready to eat lunch. Toddlers Wash hands and some get diaper change. Toddlers all eat together. The program serve family style. Some toddlers know how to serve themselves. Toddlers are trained to take their plates and place them in the container. After eating toddlers had their hands washed and diapers changed. Mats were put down and each mat has a blanket. Toddlers were not allowed to take their shoes off. The toddler area is setup like a school, which I thought was not appropriate for the age group.

CHAPTER XVIII

OBSERVATION RESULTS

1. All centers were set up like schools. All centers have classrooms and are equipped like schools. Home child care has home environment settings.

2. The lesson plans at the centers were to structured. Home child care has a monthly curriculum that they follow, which is a smoother transition throughout the day.

3. Children at centers have a variety of choices but are rushed through them because the program must follow a daily schedule Home child gives the children a variety of choices and are not rushed through them. They can spend weeks on a project if they want.

4. Children are not allowed to remove their shoes during the day. In home child care the children are allowed to remove their shoes when they feel the need.

5. Most centers have a dress code. In home child care there is no dress code. The provider can wear jogging pants and a sweat shirt, making it easier to get involved in activities with the children.

6. Older children cannot play with their younger siblings in centers. In home child care the children can play with their younger siblings.

7. Private centers do not qualify for the Food Program. Children bring their own lunches. In home child care the children are served hot lunches because they qualify to be in the Food Program plus an extra food program through the Food Bank.

8. In centers the teacher/child ratio is high 1/12. In home child care the ratio is low, 1/6.

9. Centers are open from 6:30a.m. to 5:30p.m. daily. Home child car are opened longer hours, some 23 hours and weekends.

10. Most centers I observed did not take children shoes off before napping. In home child car the children are allowed to take their shoes off whenever they feel like it.

11. Most centers I observed do not take children out on fields trips. Home child care takes their children on field trips. The reason the centers do not take children out of their premises is because of liability insurance.

12. Some centers do not take children on nature walks because of liability insurance. In home child care the children are taken for a walk often. Even the babies are taken on strollers.

13. Some centers serve frozen meals, which I believe is not to healthy for the children. In home child care the children are served hot nutritional meals.

14. Children are not supervised well when going to the bathroom in centers. Especially if centers are located in churches.

15. Centers that are located in churches have church members walking in and out of the church where the child care center is operating. Some of these people are ex prisoners that are working as custodians.

16. Children that attend child care in schools do not look as happy as children in home child care.

17. Children attending after school child care for another 4 hours besides school time, will experience burn out in the third or fourth grade, because of the long hours of school plus the 4 hours of child care.

18. In centers siblings are separated by age. In home child care siblings are together because of the small ratio.

19. Children can bond with the provider. In centers children can not bond with the teacher because she does not have time to sit with him and talk about his every day experiences, as do the providers.

20. Children in homes have the home environment setting. Children in centers experience the class settings which are structured.

21. Children in home child care have other people they can relate to as uncle, auntie, Nana, Tata, cousins, nicknames called by other people living in the home. At a center the children can only relate with the teachers, which they need to be called a certain way.

22. Home child care is furnished like a home. Centers are furnished like a school.

23. Home child care is located in neighborhoods. Centers are located in schools, large buildings, churches, etc.

24. Home child care programs are houses. Centers are large structured buildings.

25. Children can say, "I'm going to Nana's house to play", and not, "I'm going to school to play."

26. Home child care program has family oriented settings and a center does not.

27. Home child care program, children can help set up for breakfast, lunch, or dinner and eat with the family. Children are included as part of the family unit. In centers you don't have that opportunity to eat family style meals with family members.

28. In home child care programs, children have the opportunity of having a big brother or big sister experience, which most children need. In centers they do not have that opportunity.

29. In home child care programs the children that arrive from school have the opportunity to take a nap, take their shoes off and relax or go outside and play. In centers the children that arrive from regular school do not have that opportunity. The children must participate in the activity that's going on at the time.

30. In after school childcare programs on school grounds children are on school ground from 7:00a.m. to 6:00p.m. every day five days a week. This is to much for young children. Sooner or later they start experiencing school burn-out.

CHAPTER XIX

THE IMPORTANCE OF CHILDCARE IN A HOME ENVIRONMENT SETTING

Everything I explained in this book is for you to follow at home with your child. Remember that you must take a class in CPR. That is the best gift you can give to your child. Children tend to get into things that can choke them or hurt them in some way or another and you must be prepared to help your child at that moment. The classes are given through different agencies in your community. One of the agencies is the Red Cross. They are always having CPR Classes in English and Spanish. Call your county Resource and Referral Agency they have the numbers of all the agencies that offer CPR. The book will help you decide if you want to place your child in a home childcare program or a daycare center. The decision is yours. Personally I prefer home daycare because of the family values and because children do not need to be in a structured place where it looks like a school for 10 hours a day. Children need to be in a home environment where they see family and become part of it. It should be a place where children can learn about life and nature through exploration and playing with other children. They need to be relaxed and learn values that will stay with them throughout their lives. Centers tend to lack family values because of the high ratio between teachers and children. Children are taught school readiness, but there is no closeness between the staff and children.

Children at the early ages need to develop foundation that will be with them for the rest of their lives. A good foundation with family values and a good learning safe environment is the perfect recipe for a child. I am an advocate of home childcare. I believe that home childcare that is license and the provider is attending child development training is the best place for a child. I also believe that some day all centers will be in homes located in your neighborhood. These homes will be centers but with a home setting environment. The centers will have a living room with sofas, bedrooms will have beds, kitchens will have tables where children can sit and eat a family style meal. I truly feel that someday this will happen. I see it happening now, centers try to set up an area that has a sofa and throw pillows but yet the rest of the center looks like a school. The whole place needs to have the home atmosphere or else it does not work. Right now centers are being built as one large warehouse and is separated into learning areas. Children sleep on mats, awakening to a school structured building, instead of awakening to a home setting environment to where they feel relaxed and feel they belong. Infants, toddlers, and preschoolers are to young to be placed in centers that are too structured like schools. Children become aggressive, frustrated, and become fighters, when they are placed in a school environment setting at a very young age. They tend to suffer "burnout" when they get to second, and third grade. It is sad to see this happen to children that do not deserve to go through this. This is needless, children do not have to go through this "burnout" stage if only they would have been placed in a home childcare where they learned family values and grow up with a kind family that helped them develop appropriately. The conclusion is that children need family values. They need a place where they can be themselves and depend on family to help them meet their needs. When I see children calling the caregiver by a nick name for example: Nana, grandma, auntie, etc. makes me feel that the child is in the right place. He is in a place that cares and loves him/her. Remember children of today are the leaders of tomorrow. If those children do not have family values and cannot remember the joy of being a child, what will they have to offer the world? An empty heart.

CHAPTER XX

HEALTH & SAFETY ISSUES

Kitchen Hygiene

The risk of illnesses and injuries would be reduced if you follow simple hygiene tips. Make sure you wash your dishes in the dishwasher or ¼ cup of bleach to a gallon of water. Bleach is the only solution that kills 99% of viruses, and communicable diseases. Use the bleach solution in the area where you change diapers regularly. Mop your bathroom and kitchen areas daily with the bleach solution. Wash your child's mouth toys, put them in the dishwasher. Disinfect your child's crib and change the sheets at least once a week. Always be aware of food and toys thrown on the floor. Vacuum everyday, if possible do it twice a day. This eliminates germs to build up. Children must eat healthy, clean foods. They are in the growing stage so they need foods that are nourishing to their bodies. If you, as the parent, do not do this for your own child, what makes you think someone else will? You must take care of your baby the best you can. That child is your pride and joy. Poor hygiene habits can get you and your family into big trouble. Your children can become ill regularly, and can be frustrating if you cannot figure out why Johnny is getting sick all of the time. Make sure you store your foods in the refrigerator right after you use them. Don't leave any food on the counter over night especially during the summer. Remember most food poisoning cases come from not storing the food properly.

Daily Health Checkup

Your child should be given a health check up every day before he enters the program.

A good program will have someone greeting the parents and doing a health checkup. You should do this check up with your child every morning before taking him/her to childcare.

The daily health checkup includes the following:

1. Face: Is it hot or cold when you pad it?
2. Eyes: Are they red, runny or have thick sleep on the bottom eye lid?
3. Skin: Is there bruises, bites, sores, rash, etc.
4. Nose: Is it runny? Does it have thick mucus?
5. Mouth: Does the mouth have blisters? Does it have open sores inside and outside the mouth. Check to see if the child has a cough.
6. Throat: Is it red? Is the child complaining about a sore throat?
7. Chest: Check to see if there is any wheezing, and slow breathing,
8. Neck: Check to see if his neck does not hurt. Touch the glands to see if they are not swollen.

Always wash your child's hands before eating, after using the toilet, after they have touched someone that is sick, and after playing outside. Check the center's daily schedule and see if they posted washing hands throughout the day. If they don't include hand washing on their daily routine then perhaps you need to remind them children must wash their hands throughout the day.

How To Handle Food Storing

The most important thing to know is how to handle food-borne bacteria that gets people sick. Share this with your childcare provider.

1. If you practices poor personal hygiene
2. Failure to maintain room temperature foods
3. Preparation of foods that are more than two days old. Remember germs d not change the look of foods.
4. Most food borne illnesses are from foods that were stored improperly.

Handling Foods

1. Do not wash your hands in the same sink you are washing your vegetable or meats
2. Do not prepare foods if you are sick or have open sores.
3. Do not touch your nose or mouth while cooking.
4. Do not touch the area of a glass or cup when used for drinking.
5. Do not buy cans that are dented
6. Store foods below 40 degree Fahrenheit
7. Offer nutritional foods for your child to taste

Hand-Washing Procedures

Share this process with your provider.
1. Always use soap and warm water
2. Rub your hands as you wash them
3. Rinse your hands thoroughly
4. Dry your hands with a clean paper towel

Diaper Changing Procedures

Share this information with your provider. This is very important if Your child is an infant.
1. Never leave a child by himself
2. Check on the items you need to clean the infant. Make sure they are close by.
3. Place baby on the diapering area.

4. Use gloves when removing soiled diaper, remember a girl you start from the top down when wiping.
5. Place soiled diaper and wipes in a bag and tie.
6. Remove gloves and wash your hands with soap and warm water
7. Clean and disinfect the diapering area.

Crib Changing Procedures

1. Clean mattress with disinfectant weekly
2. Change sheets once a week or when soil

Field Trips

Make sure the program your child is in follow the procedures when taking a field trip. You as a parent have the right to ask questions about the field trip. You can ask the following questions.

1. What is the teacher/child ratio? One teacher per six children.
2. Does the program have liability insurance? Please ask to see it.
3. Does the car have enough car seats available?
4. Does the car have seat belts that are functional and in good condition?
5. Are you taking an emergency folder with all the children names and phone numbers?
6. Is there a plan in place in case the vehicle breakdown?
7. Do you have a first aid kit in all the vehicles transporting children?
8. Are the activities during the field trip age appropriate?
9. Am I signing a permission letter?
10. Are the volunteers that are going on the field trip parents? Of children attending the program?
11. Are you taking an emergency box with food, water, blankets, flashlights, radio.

Emergency Plan at home

1. Always have an evacuation Plan posted at home and make sure the childcare the child is attending has one posted.
2. Always have an emergency trash can at home filled with items that are needed in case of emergency occurs(Blankets, food, water, radio, batteries, flashlight)
3. Make sure the childcare has an emergency trash can filled with items for in case of an emergency occurs.
4. Practice fire drills, earthquake drills, flood drills, at home
5. Make sure the childcare where your child is attending practice the fire drills, earthquake drills once a month. The form must be posted and signed.
6. Prepare a folder with important documents and put them somewhere you can grab them if needed.
7. After an earthquake shut off the gas meter. Know where you have the wrench and practice on how to turn the valve off.

Drowning Prevention

Most children from the age of 1 to 4 drown at home in the backyard pool. Most children are in the care of their parents or provider. Always fence your pool area and make sure the childcare provider's pool is fenced and locked at all times.

Children under the age of one drown at home in bathtubs. Make sure you are always present. Remember there have been children drowning in wading pools with just one inch of water.

Car Seat Safety

The proper use of the car seat will prevent injuries to your child. Infants weighing under 20 pounds must be secured properly in car seat and must be rear facing position in the car. When your child weighs over 20 pounds he/she must be placed in a car seat facing forward but in the back seat of the car. When your child is 40 to 80 lbs. he/she must be in a booster chair. Remember: Never leave your child alone in the car!

If your child rides a school bus:
Teach your child to wait for the bus in a safe area. He/she must be able to see the bus driver. He/she must wait until the driver gives him a signal to enter. Tell your child to stay seated while the bus is moving and do not distract the driver. Stay quiet and do not talk to the driver unless something

Out of the ordinary is happening to your child.

CHAPTER XXI

SAFETY AT HOME

Use the outlet covers in all electrical outlets in your house. Children tend to put bobby pins into the outlets and in the process get electrical shock.

Be aware of toys on the floor. You can trip and get injured. Get rid of broken toys. Your child can get injured and you! Check your provider home for broken toys. Make her aware of the danger of having broken toys. Tell her you don't want your child to get hurt. Does your home have smoke detectors in every room? Make sure your home has them. It prevents fires from spreading. Smoke detectors are inexpensive. They cost approximately $10-$12. Also carbon monoxide detectors are important to install. They will alert you if there is a leak of carbon monoxide in the house. Install them close to the bedrooms. Carbon monoxide does not smell and cannot be seen, but can kill you.

Alert your provider about carbon monoxide. Tell her to install them if she does not have them. The detectors are inexpensive. They can be bought a Home Depot. Your home should have a fire extinguisher near your kitchen.

You never know if you'll ever need it. Most fires start in the kitchen.

Install safety latches in your kitchen and throughout your home. Children explore with medicines and dangerous products.

Share with your provider all the information I shared with you. Make her aware the importance of having her house safe for your child and the other children under her care. Even though the provider is license they tend to forget to follow the rules and regulations of the state. Providers are hard working women. Sometimes they take their job for granted that they over see important regulations that must be followed by all that are license by the Department of Social Services Community Care License. It does not make the provider a bad person it just that they over work themselves and tend to forget, so you are there to remind them of the importance to follow the rules and regulations of the state. Thank them for doing a great job taking care of your child. Tell them you are not reporting her but trying to help her get back on track.

As a parent you have the right to tell her what you see wrong. Tell her in a nice tone of voice. She will appreciate your concern. If she does not resolve the problem and continues to ignore your concern, you have the right to report her to licensing and terminate your contract with her. Most of the time the provider will listen and resolve the problem immediately. Most providers do not want any problems with licensing. Remember this is their job, they are getting paid to take care of children. Your child is the most important person in your life and you are the only one that can speak out for him/her.

They depend on you!

CHAPTER XXII

CONCLUSION

Infants and toddlers need to trust the person that is caring for them. Once the child has developed the trust than she is ready to explore and learn. The environment setting is very important in a child's life. Is she comfortable in that environment? Is the environment safe and spacious? Infants and toddlers need to be in an environment that looks and feels like home. They do not need to be in centers where there is ten other babies plus ten other toddlers being cared for. At that age children need one on one attention. Home childcare provides that. The personal attention that a child needs at that age. This is the Trust vs Mistrust stage that infants and toddlers must master before going into the Independence stage. I don't think that infants and toddlers master Trust vs Mistrust stage fully when they are in centers. Centers tend to change staff constantly. Especially when they are under staff.

Centers move staff around when the teacher/child ratio is not under compliance with the state and federal regulations.

Most centers are funded by the state and federal agencies. They only care about being under compliance and care less for the infants and toddlers emotions. Infants and toddlers need the same caregiver throughout the day. They do not need to see a new face every two hour. Some centers are trying.

To keep the same caregiver for the infants and toddler, but it's impossible due to lack of qualified staff. In a home childcare program the infants and toddlers have two caregivers caring for them. The same caregiver throughout the day. Also the ratio is quite small in a home childcare setting.

A small home childcare program has the limit of having 2 infants and 4 toddlers. In a center they can have 4 infants and twelve toddlers in one area and 4 infants and twelve toddler in another area, with qualified staff.

Infants and toddlers need the closeness with the caregiver. The hugs and tender massages that they deserve and want. They do not need the loud voices and confusion that is going on in large centers.

When the child gets to the age of 18 months they start to develop independence. They get a greater sense of autonomy. The child starts to climb, talk, and is able to say "no" when he feels he doesn't want something to happen. He stands up for his rights. He becomes independent and loves it.

The stage is Independence vs shame and doubt.

At home childcare they are able to express themselves a lot more then at a childcare center. At the childcare center you are told to sit quietly and do what the teacher tells you to do. It is to structure for a child. At a home childcare program they let them talk all the time and let them solve problem, unless it's something serious, than the caregiver takes charge. The children in home childcare programs are not placed in a structured program but a choice program. They have a choice of what they want to do and don't have to finish the project in one day if they don't feel like it. Home childcare is like a family unit. Children become part of the family unit they are placed in. The family involves them in all activities going on within the family. The children learn family values that will stay with them throughout their lives.

At centers children don't have that. Yes, they are taught about family but they are not involved in family values throughout the day. Centers are trying to teach children family values through family pictures, poster of families, posters of different jobs that the children can relate to, but are missing the most important element, being able to go through the emotions and actions of developing family values. Children need nurturing and caring at an early age. They need to be hugged and their needs met. Most centers are worried about the paperwork and cleaning the center that they tend to forget the importance of helping the child develop properly. In home childcare there is no paperwork from the state or federal that must be kept up daily. The providers do have the food program forms that must be done at the end of the month but not observations like the centers must do every day on each child. Home childcare is a place where children can be children. They want to take a long nap they can, if they want to take their shoes off during nap they can, if they want to eat extra food and there is left overs they can, if they want to call the caregiver a special name for example nana, mama, grandma, etc. they can. In daycare centers the children must call all the teachers and assistants by their first name. No nick names are allowed.

At the age of 4 the children start to develop a sense of initiative rather than guilt. They say "I have a great idea". "Why don't we do this instead of that"

They don't feel guilty for not choosing the other. Children need to get involved in fantasy play with others. They need to get stronger in social skills. Learn to ask questions and demand answers. This stage is called Initiative vs Guilt.

At the age of 6 children start to develop a sense of industry rather than inferiority. Children start to feel "I can do that" rather than I'm having fear "I can't do that". It is a time when children are learning to write, read, ride a bike. He feels good about himself. He feels he can do things on his own and most of the time mastering the task. This stage is Industry vs. Inferiority

In centers children are into art activities. Art activities that are send home so that parents can see that the children are learning. At a home childcare program they are more active in motor skills (large and small), so they have a better chance of developing the stage Industry vs Inferiority.

In home childcare children play outdoors and indoors longer than childcare centers. They are given the chance of developing physical skills, emotional skills, social skills, and cognitive skills just by playing with others. They do art activities twice a month to where centers do art activities almost every day. Centers worry that parents think that their children are not learning, so centers want to show the parents that children are learning through art. The art is send home daily.

Parents know, if their children are happy being there than they don't worry about work send home. Parents know that there will be time for school work as they get older. Parents want their children to develop physically, emotionally, socially, and cognitively strong. At 2 to 4 years old parents want their children to be in a safe environment and some place where they are having fun. They don't worry about home work because they know that it comes later.

Erikson was a psychologist and psychoanalyst that was right on the stages of developments. He believed that children go through stages and go in and out of that stage until they master that certain stage of development.

Children can go on to another stage but comes back to the stage that was not fully mastered, and masters it. Erikson developed 8 stages of development:

Trust vs. Mistrust, Independence vs. shame and doubt, Initiative vs. Guilt, Industry vs. Inferiority, Identity vs. Role Confusion, Intimacy vs. Isolation, Generativity vs Self Absorption, and Integrity vs. Despair. I explained the first four stages of development because I felt that was important for you to know. We are discussing infants and toddlers not adults.

Children have nine temperament traits. They are Activity level, Biological rhythms, Approach/withdrawal, Adaptability, Quality of mood, Intensity of reactions, Sensitivity threshold, Distractibility, and Persistence.

Knowing these traits helps you to know your child temperaments, and you will be able to help him and yourself on what kind activities are good for him. Activity level: Some babies are active than others. They kick and roll around. Toddlers run a lot and don't stand still for no one. Some babies are very mellow and are not active at all. This does not mean that they are slow learners. It just mean their temperaments are different. Regularity level:

Some babies get into a daily routine easily, but other babies do not.

Some babies will eat, sleep and defecate on a daily routine but others won't.

Adaptability: Some babies adapt changes in a smooth transition, and others do not.

Approach or withdrawal: Some babies are happy to try something new, and others hold back. Some babies laugh at their first bath but others cry.

Physical sensitively: Some babies sense what is around them.

Sounds, touch, lights all are sensitive to most babies. Some babies seem unaware of sounds, touch, and lights that surround them.

Intensity of reaction: Some babies cry very loud. Some babies are calm and cry very soft.

Distractibility: Some babies cry loud when they are hungry and some babies will quiet down when given a pacifier.

Positive or negative mood: Some babies are always smiling and seem happy at all times, but some babies will show unhappiness through crying at any moment.

Persistence: Some babies will play with a toy for a long time and some babies will change toys constantly. Some babies become bored with one toy and quickly pick up another. Some babies will stick with the same toy even though it's difficult to play with.

Go through all the traits I explained and grade your child. The scale will be from 1-5 One being regular and 5 being irregular. You will learn what kind of activities are appropriate for your child. For example if your child is regular than you give him the type of activity the child needs. If the child falls in the middle you try to comfort him with a little of both activities to see what he becomes comfortable with. Some children are calm and not active and some children are loud and active, so you need to supply the calm child with activities that are quiet maybe books, puzzles, legos, etc. while the other child that is loud and active maybe give him a ball he can kick around or ride bikes, etc.

The scale of temperament traits is excellent in finding out what your child is comfortable with and can learn at his own pace. It will make your child happy to try a new project when it's presented to him according to his temperament.

Here are some tips for you as a parent to bond with your child.

1. Do not prop your child with the bottle. Always sit on a chair and hold your baby to do bottle feeding.
2. Read books on child development so that you become knowledgeable
3. Respect your baby's needs.
4. Be there physically to touch and hold your baby.
5. Slow down your own activities for your baby sake.
6. Always make eye contact with your child.
7. Learn your baby's signals and meet his needs
8. Massage you child when you have some time.
9. Talk to your child with a mellow voice. Don't yell
10. Read and sing to your child.
11. Keep your child healthy and clean at all times. Dress your child according to the weather.
12. Again take a CPR (Cardiac Pulminary Recessitation) class. Best gift you can give your child!

Home childcare is a place your child can grow healthy and happy. The caregiver and your child will bond forever. As your child grows into adulthood he will remember the good times he had at childcare. Home childcare is like having family around while mom and dad work. Mom and dad do not have the means to teach family values to their child during the week while they work. Mom and dad can reinforce the family values in the evening and weekends when their child is with them.

Throughout my book I spoke about home childcare providers that are attending college and trainings. These providers are caring and loveable toward the children they care for. They know how critical it is for the child under their care to receive the nurturing they need at an early age. They are license through DSS community care licensing. The providers are also business orientate. They love their small business, so they continue to improve their business in every way possible. The home childcare providers that I observed are just that, women that love what they do. Women that are continuing their education and improving their business. All ten home childcare providers are women that worry when the children under their care are not eating well, are not feeling well, or not socializing with the other children.

Never hire nannies to take care of your children. Nannies do not have the training to take care of children. They do not have the knowledge of child development. Most nannies do not have any education at all. They are women that want a quick job that does not require a license or a life scan. Anyone can be a nanny with little bit of lies and a convincing manner, she will be hired by desperate working parents quickly. The reason nannies are hired by parents is because they go to their home to babysit and some even stay and live with them, which makes parents feel convinced that it's the way to go.

Nannies do not have to be license or fingerprinted, but you can send her to get fingerprinted. A life scan may cost you $75 to $100 depends where you send her to get the life scan. Call your county resource and referral program. They are able to guide you.

The new home childcare providers of the future, are women who care and believe in their business. They want to be known as professionals not just as babysitters, but as professional home childcare providers. They want to have a voice in legislation, they want to be involved in new laws that affect their business. The providers are getting more involve than ever, by attending meetings, trainings, state and local conferences. Some have gone to Washington D.C. to show their concerns on childcare issues. These are strong business women that care about their business and about the children they care for.

I remember when I first started I researched the local childcare providers around my county. I found that every one of them lacked training in early childhood. I became concerned so I started a support group. Within the year I picked up over two hundred childcare providers. I started trainings in childcare and child development. I did free trainings for nine years because I cared. As a childcare provider myself, I cared for the children that were taken care by these providers. I worried for these children health and safety.

My main concern is the safety of the children. Are different people walking into the childcare program throughout the day? Who are these people? Are they relatives or friends? Are the children being looked after when others are visiting? If I see people coming in and out of the house I get this feeling there is something else going on besides caring for the children. The children are caring for themselves not by the provider. So I instantly investigate the situation. 99% of the time I am right, something else is going on besides caring for the children.

Another main concern are the children eating healthy meals? Are the providers preparing healthy meals or are they making sandwiches and campbell's soup every day for the children? The federal government reimburses the provider for every meal they serve the children, so the children must be eating healthy meals every day. Once in a while I'll fine a provider that is not following the food program regulations. She is not serving nutritional meals. I make her feel guilty why she is keeping all the monies that should be for the children. She will pay a bill or two with that money instead of using it on the children.

My four most important points about childcare is the following:

1. Safety of the children. Is there to many people coming in and out?
2. Nutrition: Are the children getting a well balance meal every day?
3. Hygiene: Are the children noses being wiped when they have a runny nose with different tissue every time?
4. Pre-school program: If all of the above is followed daily than pre-school learning comes easy to the children.

I know that your child will be happier in a home setting learning environment. The providers are not just babysitters, they are pre-school teachers that are educated and love teaching and nurturing children. A childcare provider is a teacher, nurse, mom, grandmother, to the children under their care. They are women that are there for their children that cry because mom left them at childcare and won't be back until late afternoon, maybe ten hours later. They are women that bond with the children, so they hurt when their children are suffering, emotionally, or physically. In childcare centers, you can't bond with the children like childcare providers can. Maybe it's because pre-school teachers cannot show favoritism toward one child since the ratio between teacher and child is larger than a home childcare program. At a home childcare you can call the provider nana, mommy, grandma or other nick names, and at a childcare centers you need to call the staff by their first name. Maybe it's because the environment at a home childcare is family oriented. The family gets involved with the children. The children become part of the family. The program is in a home with a family, not in a big building that has been divided into many learning centers that are too structured like a school. So the conclusion is simple and clear, home childcare is the best place for your children to be at the age 0 to 4 years old, because of the family environment, the nurturing and family values that are practiced every day.

It's simple and clear!

Go out and choose the right program for your precious child!

Home Childcare

www.ingramcontent.com/pod-product-compliance
Lightning Source LLC
LaVergne TN
LVHW092051060526
838201LV00047B/1347